The Best Use of

Landscape Items

in Architectural Rendering

A k i r a   R y u

私が社会に出て，最初に担当したのは飲食産業会社の企画宣伝室の仕事でした。入社後，すぐにその企画宣伝室でクリエイティブな作業に取りかかったのですが，そこではアイデアを提議するには，文章だけではなくビジュアル的要素で表現することが要求されていました。つまり，アイデアを具体的に表現してみせる記号としてのスケッチが，非常に重要なものだったのです。

現代とは違い，当時はポラロイドカメラやコピー機，あるいはパソコンなどのハイテク機器など何もない時代でした。そのために，建設や増築計画案などが生まれると，すぐさま現場に立ち，周囲の関係をスケッチブックにおさめ，専門家たちの提案建物本体を完成予想図画としてまとめたものでした。

その絵はこれからはじめられる計画のイメージであって，すぐにできあがる代物ではありません。それゆえ，スケッチという観点からのみとらえた暗中模索時代の私の表現技術も，その時点ではなんとか役に立ったものです。しかし，本格的決定のとき

に，プロのレンダラーが描いた精密描写画を見て驚愕し，おおいにその道に啓蒙されたのです。

その後，私は仕事がら合流していった工芸界や店舗商業施設設計業界で企画設計，作図作画作業をつづけ，やがて独立。そしてデザイン事務所を設立して，商業施設設計・ショップインテリア設計に従事したのですが，一人二役の忙しい毎日でした。誰も助けてくれず，相手もなく，独学によって表現と画風を自然につかみ，いつのまにかスケッチ稼業が私の本業となっていました。

本書は，そんな私の実践のなかから生まれた作品集です。本書には，短時間仕上げの作風のものから，ていねいに描き込みされたもの，あるいはエクステリア，インテリアスペースなど様々な作品がおさめられています。これらの作品を紹介しながら，そのつどパースデザインのチェックポイントを解説し，同時に主要作品の基本的スケッチの作画段階を画材と実技をあわせて解説しています。また，同時にクライアントに対する心がまえや作画の段取りをも解説しています。

本書の作品と解説が，これからパースデザインを学ぶ人たちに対して何かのお役に立てれば，幸いです。

Introduction

When I started my career, I worked for the planning and publicity department of a company in the food industry. Immediately after joining the company, I started creative work in that department. According to the policy of the company at that time, in order to propose an idea, it was not enough to simply use documents; it was also necessary to use visual methods, that is to say, to make a presentation utilizing sketches to concretely express or convey one's ideas to others.

Unlike today, high-tech devices such as Polaroid cameras, copy machines and personal computers were not available. Hence, if there was a plan for a new construction project or an addition to a building, I used to go to the proposed site immediately to draw sketches. I would draw the sites themselves, and their surroundings, and then prepare predicted as-built perspectives, which always had to be attached to bid proposal documents submitted for projects designed by architects.

The perspectives that I created were utilized as a means to create images of the projects being planned, and a long time was usually needed before the projects could be realized. Therefore, even the sketches that I prepared using my unestablished expression techniques were somewhat useful. In the meantime, I was surprised by the detail and precision of the perspectives that were drawn and presented by professional renderers for developing the project images, and I was fairly enlightened by them.

After that, I continued my work in designing and planning works in industrial design and commercial facility design. Finally, I established my own design office, which was devoted primarily to the design of commercial building/facilities and shop interiors. I was very busy at that time; I had no partner to help me, and I was trying to establish my own design expressions and personal style of painting. Before I knew it, I was drawing sketches at a professional level.

This booklet contains a collection of works that I have created using the techniques that I have obtained through my experience of actual drawing. There are works which were drawn and finished in a short time, there are more detailed, precise drawings, and there are an assortment other types of exterior and interior drawings. These drawings and works are presented so that I can offer a detailed explanation the important checkpoints for drawing perspectives, and summarize the fundamental steps involved in drawing them. At the same time, I would also like to explain how we should respond to requests coming from clients, and what kinds of preparation are necessary in relation to drawing materials, skills, and other matters. I dearly hope this book will be valuable to those who wish to learn perspective design.

┌─────────────────┐
│　目　　　次　　│
└─────────────────┘

┌─────────────────┐
│ C o n t e n t s │
└─────────────────┘

┌───────┐
│ 0 0 2 │
└───────┘
まえがき
Introduction

第1章│ウォーターフロント ● Chapter 1│Waterfront　　│009

┌───────┐
│ 0 1 0 │
└───────┘
マリンレジャーワールド
海辺の大屋根のある総合イベント空間
Marine leisure world
A large-roofed multi-purposed Event Hall

┌───────┐
│ 0 1 4 │
└───────┘
大都市圏のベイエリア再生
ウォーターフロントの一大マーケットリゾート
Development of bay area in the metropolitan city
One large market resort at the waterfront

┌───────┐
│ 0 1 8 │
└───────┘
防潮閘門整備計画
市民の憩いの散策プロムナード
A tide gate completion project
Strolling promenade for relaxation of citizens

┌───────┐
│ 0 2 0 │
└───────┘
フィッシュ・マーケット・ビレッジ
ファミリー対象のショッピング＆レジャー施設
Fish market village
Family shopping mall and leisure center

┌───────┐
│ 0 2 4 │
└───────┘
海産物センター
漁港整備プラン──ファミリー向けの海岸プロムナード
Marine products center
Fishing port completion plan, family seaside promenade

第2章｜市街地開発 ●Chapter 2｜Urban development　029

0 3 0

市街地の再開発
地下街コンコースの中央広場と百貨店への人の流れを表現
Redevelopment of suburban area
Flow of people who are entering to the central plaza of the underground concourse and the depa
and the department store

0 3 2

アーケード新設計画
商店街活性化のためのグレードアップ計画
Construction project of arcade
Grade-up project to vitalize the shopping mall

0 3 6

無人搬送立体地下駐車場計画
繁華街の地下に設置する大型地下駐車場計画
Underground multistoried parking lot
with unmanned car guided system
Large underground parking lot built under shopping quarters

第3章｜商業施設 ●Chapter 3｜Commercial facilities　045

0 4 6

ショッピングセンターの中央プラザ
明るい日差しと草花に囲まれた開放感あふれる休憩エリアの演出
Central plaza of shopping mall
Dramatic presentation of open rest area full of ample sunlight and flowers

0 5 0

商業ビルの外周の環境整備計画
ヤング対象の飲食エリアの演出
Improvement plan for the environment
surrounding commercial buildings
Development of restaurants for the younger generation

0 5 2

中央空間のあるショッピングセンター計画
中央噴水をシンボルとした中庭の憩いの場
Plan of shopping mall with a wide plaza at its center
A patio rest area with a fountain constructed at its center

0 5 4

ターミナルビルのショッピングモール
旅行者,送迎者のためのショッピング＆飲食ゾーン
Shopping mall at the terminal building
Shopping center and restaurants for travelers and those who come to welcome them
or see them off

0 5 6

ファッションビル
感覚産業が集約するファッションビル
Fashion building
Fashion building occupied by fashion business enterprises

[0 6 0]

商店街アーケード計画
新興商店街に対抗する旧商店街通りの復興

Arcade construction plan for the shopping mall
Restoration of old shopping mall to compete with a new shopping area

[0 6 4]

アーケード・リニューアル計画
青空が見える開閉天井を設けたモダンな商店街

Renewal project of arcade
Modern shopping mall featuring an opening and closing type are with a ceiling that reveals the sky

[0 6 6]

ホテル内の高級レストラン
ホテル内ラウンジのような欧州風レストランルーム

A deluxe restaurant in a hotel
European-type restaurant that resembles the lounge of a hotel

[0 7 0]

ショッピングセンター・エントランス
正面入口のドアデザインの検討スケッチ

Entrance to a shopping mall
Sketch for reviewing of the entrance door design

[0 7 4]

商業ビル
中央大吹き抜けの空間をもつハイファッションビル

Commercial building
High fashion building with a large well-hole at its center

第4章│公共施設●Chapter 4│Public facilities

[0 8 8]

学園都市文化交流センター
交流学生室, 実技研修室内から学生食堂をのぞむ

Cultural exchange center in a college town
View of a cafeteria from an exchange student's room and a study and training room

[0 9 2]

欧州風郊外学園計画
欧州風の美しい学園キャンパスと池のある中央庭園の展開

European style suburban college town
Development of beautiful European style campus and central garden with a pond

[0 9 4]

カルチャーセンター
自然に親しめる長期滞在住居ゾーン

Culture center
Nature-conscious residential for extended stays

098

ターミナル地下街コンコース
自然採光あふれる大円形吹き抜けアトリウムをもつ地下コンコース

Underground concoourse at a terminal building
Underground concourse with a large circular well-hope atrium allowing the entry of natural lighting

100

レジャー施設内の大温室
大ジャングル庭園＆カフェ休憩所のある光景

A large greenhouse in a leisure facility
A large jungle garden and a cafe

第5章｜住宅●Chapter 5｜Residential houses

109

110

休暇住宅村
海の休暇住宅分譲計画

Resort residence village
Parceling-out plan of seaside resort residences

114

住宅マンション
山間部にある自然林に囲まれた閑静なメゾネット

Condominium
Maisonette-type condominium surround by a quiet forest

116

リゾート地のセカンドハウス
海抜25mの岸上の景勝地に建つ休暇住宅

Villa residence in a resort area
Resort house constructed on the top of a seaside hill 25 meters above the sea level

120

セカンドハウス室内
温暖地に建つリゾートハウスのインテリア

Resort house
Interior of a resort house built in an area with a mild climate

第6章｜環境パースの主役達●
Chapter 6｜Star players in the world of landscape perspectives

129

129

人物/植物
Human figures/Plants

142

あとがき
Afterword

The Best Use of Landscape Items in Architectural Rendering
© Akira Ryu

published by Graphic-sha Pblishing Co., Ltd. 1994

ISBN4-7661-0771-3

First Edition 1994

Graphic-sha Publishing Co., Ltd.
1-9-12 Kudan-Kita, Chiyoda-ku, Tokyo 102 Japan
Phone 3-3263-4318   Fax. 3-3263-5297

Printed in Japan

第1章｜ウォーターフロント

Chapter 1｜Waterfront

マリンレジャーワールド

海辺の大屋根のある総合イベント空間

Marina leisure world

A large-roofed multi-purposed Event Hall

南側に海を取り入れた大空間のマーケット中央をアピールするため，海側からの構図にし，海にそったプロムナードなど贅沢な空間を連想するような雰囲気に仕上げることに重点をおく。この場合，一つ一つの精密な描写は必要なく，人物は粗描で植物はイメージの段階で，海風にたえる様子とか種類の選択などはあとの段階で処理をする。

設計コンセプトポイント

建築家，計画グループの考え方，設計コンセプトを十分把握することはたいへん難しい。彼ら自身の内に広がるイメージの世界を瞬時に理解し，表現することになるので，あらゆる角度から質問し，さらに討議し妥協点を見出すことが肝心。

Check point for mode of expression

To emphasize the large space central portion of the market located adjacent to the seaside to its south, consider the composition of the painting seen from the seaside; center on the creation of an atmosphere that reminds us of the luxurious space of the promenade along the seashore. In this case, it is not necessary to precisely draw the scene. During the image creation stage, draw the incidental humans and plants roughly, and then, during the final stage, precisely draw the types of trees and plants which are capable of withstanding the strong seaside breeze.

Main point of design concept

It is quite difficult to fully understand the concepts of the architect, project group and designer. As you have to catch the images and conceptions that they have of the project, and then express their images as precisely as possible, it is necessary to ask them questions from various points of views. This will open the way towards discussion with them, and will help you find an effective way to approach the rendering task.

サイズ:513mm×725mm
Size:513mm×725mm

❶全体的に，日の当たる南側から中央プラザを臨むように構成する。構図は，中央広場と海との一体感を表現したいため，海側から奥行きのあるアトリウムを中心として2Fレベルに水平視線を決める。ペン線描画として仕上げ，一番最後に着色予定の船，旗，白い柱，人物や植物などはマスキング液でふせておく。

❶ Choose the general composition of the picture in which the scenes from the south side to the central plaza in the sunshine are included. Locate the horizontal eye level at the second floor of the building centering on the atrium, which has a longitudinal depth, in order to integrate the feelings of the central plaza and the sea. Finish the line drawing and use the masking solution to cover the ships, flags, white pillars, and incidental humans and plants which are to be colored in the final stage.

❷空と海を彩色する。このときフリーハンド方式で全部すませてもよいが，美しい調子を出すためにエアブラシで空と海の水色を彩色し，その後手塗りで明暗やコントラストをつけていく。

❷ Color the sky and sea. It may be possible to color the entire picture using a freehand method, but draw the sky and sea with a light blue color beforehand using an airbrush, and then manually color the tone and the contrast of the shaded and bright portions so that fine color tone expression can be made.

❸遠くの高層ビルの彩色。中央アトリウム天井の彩色。床などの部分の第2段階の彩色へと進む。各店舗部分の彩色をする。喫茶店，飲食店，売店などの業種がわかる程度に仕上げる。

❸ Coloring of high-rise buildings in the distance. Color the ceiling of the central atrium, then color the floor in the second stage. Color the shops and paint the coffee shops and restaurants and make them stand out so that they can be vaguely be identified.

❹はじめに吹きつけた海に，さざ波や噴水，船などの反射や映り込みを描く。マスキング液でふせておいた船や人物などを専用のラバーゴムでこすり取り着色する。

❹ Draw the rippling waves, fountain and the reflections of the ships on the sea on which colors have been previously sprayed. Remove the masking solution which covers the ships and incidental humans using a special eraser, and then color them.

❺面相彩色筆（腰の強い白狸毛の筆を使用）の使い込んで，ややすれたものを使う。

❺ Use the second-hand color brush (tough white raccoon hair that has been already slightly worn.

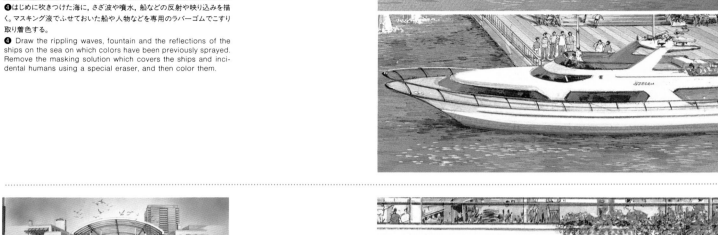

❻植栽など筆先でつつくように着色する。海上のクルーザーや人物，植物など全体の構図をもう一度見つめ，色の調子をコントロールしながらまとめる。

❻ Draw the greenery by dotting the colors with the tip of brush. Look over the entire composition of the picture once again including cruisers, incidental humans and plants, and finish the painting up by conditioning the color tone.

大都市圏のベイエリア再生

ウォーターフロントの一大マーケットリゾート

Development of by area in the metropolitan city

One large market resort at the waterfront

表現チェックポイント

全体の構図は水平線をやや高く取り，広い範囲を見渡せるようにした。都市周辺の水辺，海岸，波止場地区などの開発に伴うスケッチには，多くの景観要素が集まってくる。たとえば，商業施設としての建造空間，ガラス張りのアトリウム，広いプラザ，波止場に停泊中の豪華客船の姿，空を飛ぶ海鳥などが素材になる。

設計コンセプトポイント

完成後の賑わいや施設の繁栄を予測させる雰囲気にポイントをおく。スケッチ全体を明るい快活なものにするため，海辺の解放感，ふだん描かない入道雲やカモメなどを点景に取り入れる。

Check point for mode of expression

In deciding the composition of the perspective, select the horizontal eye line at a slightly higher level so that you can cover a wider view. Many scenery elements should be included when sketching areas along the waterfronts, seasides and wharves of metropolitan cities. Here for example, the building space for the commercial facilities, the glazed atrium, the spacious plaza, the luxury liner and birds in the sky should all be painted in.

Main point of design concept

Place priority on drawing an atmosphere which suggests that the area will soon be thriving after the completion of the project. To add a brisk feeling to the entire sketch, the relaxed feeling of the seaside, i.e., the gigantic columns of clouds in the sky and the seagulls should be drawn in as incidental items.

サイズ:338mm×620mm
Size:338mm×620mm

❶全体の構図を考えながら，ペン線描画として仕上げる。
❶ Finish the line drawing taking the entire composition into consideration.

❷空の着色は，自由に表現する。海の色は，濃いマリンブルーで印象を強くする。
❷ Express the sky as you like. The sea should be drawn in dark blue colors to intensify the impression.

❸ブルー系の着彩は，薄い色から濃い色までの段階で，順次着色していく。
❸ When drawing with the blue system colors, use lighter colors first and then proceed gradually with heavier colors.

❹広場の床面を第一段階の基礎塗りをする。
❹ Draw the floor of the plaza roughly in the first stage.

❺店や売店を暖色系で彩色する。完成に近づいたところで構図をもう一度よく考えて、大きな植物の色と人物の色などで全体のバランスを整える。人の歩くところやペーブメントなどは, 白っぽい面積が広すぎて調子が合わなければ, 少々色の変化をつけてみるのもよい。
❺ Color the shops and stands with warm colors. When drawing comes to an end, review the entire composition again to adjust the entire balance, including the colors of plants and incidental humans. The passage and pavement where people are to walk can be slightly colored if the white area looks large and unbalanced in the picture.

防潮閘門整備計画
市民の憩いの散策プロムナード

A tide gate completion project
Strolling promenade for relaxation of citizens

表現チェックポイント

広大な面積にわたるスケッチは，鳥瞰図画で描けば全体景観が一目でわかるようになる。周囲環境は参考写真と地図でデッサン描写する。時間があれば精密な作画も考えられるが，短時間に仕上げるためにはペン線描画で仕上げ，彩色する方法がベスト。海の部分のみをエアブラシで吹きつけたのち，手塗りで水彩画風に着色していく。

設計コンセプトポイント

広報パンフレットにもなることを考慮して，印刷効果のため特に海の表現にポイントをおき，仕上げた。周辺の工場，倉庫などはモノトーン（単色）で仕上げ，あくまでも中央部分の施設が絵の中心になるように心がけた。

サイズ:350mm×527mm
Size:350mm×527mm

❶まず全体の構図をかちっと決めてから，ペン線描画として仕上げていく。
❶ Decide on the entire composition in advance, and then finish the perspective in the line drawing.

Check point for mode of expression

In order to sketch the vast area here, the entire scene can be included if the birds-eye-view drawing technique is used. Sketch the peripheral environment referring to photos and maps. Though you can draw precisely if you have enough time, it is best to sketch the peripheral area using a simple line drawing technique, and then put in colors for a quick finish. After spraying only the sea portion with an airbrush, color manually as you would in a watercolor painting.

Main point of design concept

In drawing the perspective, priority was placed on the expression of the sea in anticipation of how it would appear when printed in the upcoming PR pamphlets. The plants and warehouses in the adjacent area were finished in monotone and care was taken to highlight only the facilities located in the central portion of the picture.

❷最初の作業で，絵具をつけたくないところをマスキングフイルムとマスキング液でふせてから，メインになる中央の海の表現を一気にすませる。
❷ At the initial stage, cover the areas where no coloring is required with masking film and masking solution, and then finish the drawing of sea in the center of the perspective.

❸その後，フイルムを取り除きフリーハンドで彩色する。
❸ Next, remove the masking film and place color over different areas of the composition with a free hand.

フィッシュ・マーケット・ビレッジ
ファミリー対象のショッピング＆レジャー施設

Fish market village
Family shopping mall and leisure center

表現チェックポイント

計画案成功の約束を経営者側に強くアピールするために，イメージを重視して人物などを多く描き込んで作画したもの。そのために，天井のシースルーのおおいなどは，建築的な考慮からイメージ主体の描写で表現している。

設計コンセプトポイント

一方的に表現を決めてしまうわけにはいかないので，事前にタッチや仕上がり表現の検討が必要になる。完成する画風内容を，計画グループ側によく把握してもらってからの作業になる。完成の雰囲気をよく理解してもらえてからの表現ならば，かなり個性の強いタッチでも説得力のある作品として成功といえる。

Check point for mode of expression

To effectively convince the owners or managers of the shops that the projected construction of the shopping mall and leisure center would be successful, priority was placed on the image creation of the project. Accordingly, incidental items such as people have been rendered. To achieve the objectives of the perspective, features such as the see-through coverage of the ceiling were drawn with an emphasis on expressing their forms from an architectural point of view.

Main point of design concept

Before deciding how to express the image, it is necessary for you to consult with the designer or architect about the touch and finish of the rendering. It would be better to start the actual task of painting after the objectives of the image painting have been confirmed and fully under-stood by the project group. Even a perspective with a fairly strong personal touch can be persuasive, as long as it helps everyone under-stand the atmosphere of the area after the completion of the project.

サイズ:400mm×680mm
Size:400mm×680mm

❶ペン線描画として完成させる。すでにこの段階で，絵としては完成していることになる。
❶ Complete the perspective with line drawing. The perspective should be considered as a completed painting at this stage.

❷海，空の色，そしてカフェレストランの中の床面を着色する。また，足元の影も入れる。
❷ Color the sea, sky and floors in the cafe restaurant, and shadows at the feet of incidental humans.

❸屋根，船などは，色の濃淡までを順々に彩色していく。
❸ Color such objects as roofs and ships in the order of color tone.

❹全体の調子が整えられてくると、次に人物などで色調のコントロールを図る。

❹ After the entire perspective tone has been adjusted, try to condition the perspective's color tone, adjusting the colors used for incidental humans.

❺植物の色も単なるグリーンのみではなく、光の具合などを考慮して色を変化させてることが大切。

❺ It is important to color the plants in a variety of colors, considering the effects of the light on the plants instead of painting with a single shade of green.

パーススケッチを描く道具と技法

まず構図を決めて、鉛筆線描画を本番用のキャンソンボード（白）にトレースダウンして、ロットリングペン（0.15mm）で線描画として仕上げていく。直線は三角定規（薄手のもので片手につかみ、画面上ベタにおかず、ペン先をそわす）を使い、曲線は雲形定規などを使い、正円形はロットリングペン用コンパスで描く。

エアブラシ吹きつけ着彩の場合は、色をつけたくない部分（人物や植物の幹や葉、店の商品など）にマスキング液を塗りふせをして、液が乾いたらその上から全面にマスキングフイルムを張りつけ、押さえつけたら着彩したいところをはずしエアブラシで吹きつけをする。そして、ふたたびフイルムをふせ、次の部分をはがし……という手順で根気よく繰り返し作業していく。あとは、すべてのフイルムを取り除き（マスキング液は専用ラバーゴムでこすり取ることができる）フリーハンドによる筆塗りで終える。

今回紹介している作品は、ほとんどが短時間で表現することが最優先されるプレゼンテーションのためのパーススケッチなので、その作画手法も短時間で表現することに主眼がおかれている。また、計画、設計図ができる以前に、口頭説明だけで依頼者側（計画グループ）の設計コンセプトをくみ取り、表現タッチを考えながら描写作業していくというテクニックの例でもある。

本書に掲載されている技法は、すべてこの要領で描写、作画されたものである。一部ペン線描画に見えないくらいに、たんねんに塗り込まれた作品や鉛筆線描から直接、彩色着色されたものも掲載してある。これらの技法を参考にしてほしい。

Tools and techniques for drawing perspective sketches

First of all, decide on the composition of the painting that you are to perform, and trace a pencil line sketch onto a Canson board so that it can be finished as a rottling pen (0.15mm) line drawing. Use a triangle scale when drawing straight lines. (Select a thin scale. Hold the scale down with one hand and run the pen along with the edge of the scale. Do not allow any of the triangle scale to touch the surface of the drawing paper. Try to keep one corner of the triangle scale lifted.) When drawing curved lines, use curved rules. Use a special divider for rottling pens when drawing circular forms.

When spraying color with an airbrush, apply masking liquid to the portions of the painting where coloring is not required (incidental people tree, trunks and leaves of plants, store displays, etc.), and after the masking liquid has dried up, cover it with masking film. Once the painting is entirely covered with the masking film, remove the film only in the portions where you plan to apply color with the airbrush. After the color has been sprayed to these selected portions, cover the entire painting with the masking film once more, and then remove the film over the next portion to be colored. Repeat these steps as many times as necessary until the required coloring is finished. When all the necessary portions are colored, remove all of the masking film (masking liquid can be scrubbed off with a special rubber tool) and finish the painting using freehand brushstrokes.

Since almost all of the perspective sketches introduced in this book are for presentations which had to be completed within very short periods, the techniques presented in this book can mainly be applied to quickly finished paintings. In some of the examples in this book, the illustrator listens to the designer and grasps the designer's objectives before the project plan or any of the design drawings have been prepared, and the illustrator then goes on to to draw the perspective sketches with the appropriate expressive touch.

All the perspective sketches introduced in this book have been drawn applying this technique. Some of them do not look line drawings at all; in some cases colors were carefully applied over the lines, and in other cases the works were colored immediately after the pencil line drawings were finished. Refer to these techniques when you draw your perspective sketches.

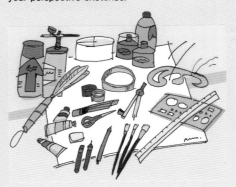

海産物センター

漁港整備プラン──ファミリー向けの海岸プロムナード

Marine products center

Fishing port completion plan, family seaside promenade

表現チェックポイント

構図は，海と親しみながら飲食シーン，鮮魚のショッピングなど海岸プロムナードでの人々の行動を表すことに重点をおき，建物本体の姿より将来の姿を連想させる景観を表現した。また，海の青さや昔からある貴重な松の緑と周辺の空間を表現できるように努力した。

設計コンセプトポイント

建造物の規模はもちろん，完成後の周辺状況を連想させるように努めた。人物の多さやプラントボックスの緑や植栽，外装を飾るフラッグ，海に接岸しているクルーザーなどを点景として取り入れて，賑やかさを出す。もしそれらを除外すると，殺風景で趣のまったくないスケッチになってしまうだろう。

サイズ:390mm×662mm
Size:390mm×662mm

❶ Color the entire sky. Spray the sea once with an airbrush to express the light blue of the sea.

Check point for mode of expression

The priority has been given to the rendering of people enjoying themselves as they shop for fresh fish, dine, drink, and delight in the scenery of the seaside promenade. In addition, emphasis was placed on the expression of the future image of the landscape instead of on the buildings themselves. Efforts were made to express the green of the old pine trees, highlighting their historical significance and interacting with the neighboring space, as well as the blue of the sea.

Main point of design concept

Efforts were made to express an atmosphere which foretells the environment of the vicinity after the completion of the promenade, as well as to express the massive scale of the building. Many incidental items are incorporated to provide a light, gay atmosphere to the picture, including people, green plant boxes, plantation, flags on the exterior of the building, and the cruiser along the berth. Without these interesting items, the sketch would be inartistic and unattractive.

❷次に、筆塗りで海にさざ波などを描き入れて、より海面らしい調子を表現する。

❷ Paint rippling waves on the sea with a brush to express the tone of the sea.

❸店の周辺や店内の様子を暖色系で彩色する。左右の松の木や街路樹も着色する。

❸ Color the shops and inside the shops with warm system colors. Color the pine trees and roadside trees on both side of the street.

❹日除けテントやデザインフラッグ、そして人物の着色をすませ、仕上げる。

❹ Color the sun visor tent, design flag and incidental humans to complete the perspective.

湖岸レジャー施設

開放的で明るく，そして人物や木もイラスト風に表現してみた。

Lake side leisure facility

Prepared with an open and light touch. Incidental
people and plants are expressed in an illustrative style.

人工磯公園計画案
（大阪市港湾局）

人工磯での魚釣り，ジョギングコース，サイクリングコースなどの
計画が説明できるように鳥瞰で描いた。
松などの植栽は数年後の成長した姿にする。

Artificial seaside park project plan
(Osaka Prefectural Government Port and Harbor Bureau)

This birds-eye view perspective was prepared so that
the plans for constructing the fishing area, the jogging
course and the cycling course could be explained at
the project presentation. Growing plants like the young
pine trees were drawn as they were expected to
appear several years later.

第 2 章 | 市 街 地 開 発

Chapter 2 | Urban development

市街地の再開発

地下街コンコースの中央広場と百貨店への人の流れを表現

Redevelopment of suburban area

**Flow of people who are entering to
the central plaza of the underground concourse and the department store**

表現チェックポイント

中央コンコースから駅へ，また百貨店への人の流れと，地下街計画を再検討するためのスケッチとして作画された。設計図面もなく，口頭説明で意図を聞き描いたものである。これは場数を踏まないと簡単にはいかないが，ショップや階段，エスカレーター，人などごく初歩段階の表現の集合体と思えばよい。このような景観は，常に自分で歩いたところを観察して，必ず頭の中に記録しておくこと。日常のちょっとした注意力が役に立つはずである。

設計コンセプトポイント

仕上がりがどういう雰囲気になるか，書き手にもわからないときがある。このような場合は，依頼者グループとよく打ち合わせて取りかかる。この種のスケッチでは，実際に見えないところを透視画で描いたり，じゃまな天井部分を消してしまうこともある。

サイズ:300mm×600mm
Size:300mm×600mm

Check point for mode of expression

This perspective has been prepared as an illustration of the flow of people heading for the department store, walking from the central concourse to the station, and as a general plan for the underground market. The execution of this illustration was based not on the design drawings, but on a verbal explanation of the project objectives. Only an experienced illustrator can successfully draw this type of illustration. Beginners should consider this as a combination of elementary expressions of various types of shops, stairs, escalators and people. This is the kind of scenery that can usually be observed when taking a walk, and if you keep this in mind and make an effort to observe and memorize the scenes of daily life, you will find this helpful in succeeding with these types of paintings.

Main point of design concept

Sometimes even the illustrator cannot imagine what the atmosphere will be like after the completion of drawing. When this is the case, the illustrator should consult with the client before starting to draw the illustration. In this type of perspective, what cannot be actually seen can be drawn. On the other hand, what can be actually seen is intentionally excluded, just as the ceiling is excluded in this illustration.

❶キャンソンボードにHB鉛筆で直接デッサンして，そのあとで本清書をする。

❶ Draw the preliminary sketches over the Canson board directly with an HB pencil, and then finish the illustration after touching up.

❷ペン線描画として描いていく。曲線は雲形定規や自在定規などを使用するといいだろう。

❷ Draw the illustration as a line drawing. For drawing the curved lines, the use of a French curve or adjustable ruler is recommended.

❸イメージ画とはいえ，美しく，そしてシャープな彩色にしたい部分はエアブラシを使用する。

❸ Though the purpose is to draw an image perspective, use an airbrush when drawing the portions where the fine and sharp color finish is necessary.

❹空やガラス張りのビル外観は，エアブラシでないとこのようなタッチにはならない。この作品はかなり濃厚な不透明絵具で着色した。

❹ Unless an airbrush is used, the touch you can see in the sky or glazed exterior of the building of this perspective cannot be painted. Thick opaque colors were used to finish this illustration

アーケード新設計画

商店街活性化のためのグレードアップ計画

Construction project of arcade

Grade-up project to vitalize the shopping mall

表現チェックポイント

夕刻から夜にかけての華やかな状態を連想させるため，夜景にした。各専門店の賑わいと夜景に発光する天井部分を強く表現した。これほどタッチの強い仕上げにするのは，クライアントに対して強力なインパクトを考慮してのこと。商業施設やイベントのスケッチなどは，インパクト性を第一に重視する。営業中のカフェ，専門店の姿，走っている車やバス，そしてメインテーマである光るアーケードなど，活気ある表現になるように留意して，準備しておかなければ短時間で勢いのある画風のスケッチはできあがらない。

設計コンセプトポイント

完成予想図を描くとき，依頼者とわれわれ描き手との間には必ず考え方の違いがある。打ち合わせ時に，描き手から率先して，構図についてのリーダーシップを取る場合がある。近年，複雑で繁雑な空間建築物の依頼が多くなった。苦手な表現技術の勉強を繰り返し，試し描きをするのが上達の早道になる。

Check point for mode of expression

The night scenery was chosen to remind the viewers of the gay atmosphere of twilight and evening in the town. The thriving specialty shops and the ceiling portion, which are illuminated at night, were highlighted. This strong touch was chosen for the expression to make a strong impact on the client. When drawing the sketches of commercial facilities or events, priority should be given to the impact of the drawing. It is impossible to draw active sketches in a short period unless consideration is given to incorporating the active elements of the main theme of the perspective, to make the overall scene lively. In this case, these elements would be the cafe in operation, the specialty shops, the running cars and buses, and the illuminated arcade.

Main point of design concept

It is normal that there is gap in the perceptions of the theme of the perspective between the client and the illustrator. Therefore, the illustrator is sometimes required to take the initiative in discussion about the composition of the perspective. Of late, requests to draw buildings with complicated architectural designs have been increasing. The best way to master the drawing of perspective is to repeatedly study the techniques of expression which have not been mastered, and to draw as many sketches as possible.

サイズ：340mm×590mm
Size:340mm×590mm

❶トレーシングペーパーでの鉛筆描きの練習，あるいは一般ケント紙に鉛筆やペン線描画としての練習が必須。キャンソンボードに鉛筆で割りつけをして，それをペン線描画にする。

❶ Practice in pencil on tracing paper, or in pencil or line drawing over the paper is necessary. Divide the canson board with a pencil for the line drawing.

❷濃い空色の着色，道路（店の明かりに照らされた部分）を描く。夜空と連立するビルは，手塗りではきれいに仕上がらないのでエアブラシの力をかりる。

❷ Paint the dark blue for the sky and draw the street (the portions that are brightened by the light coming from the shops). To paint the night sky and high-rise buildings clearly and beautifully, an airbrush should be used instead of a manual technique.

❸まだ塗りたくないところを厚手のボール紙でふせながら，目的のところへ絵具を吹きつける。

❸ With a thick board, cover the areas where painting is not required at this stage, and spray on the coloring media.

❹店舗や歩道，右手アーケードファサード部分にイエローオレンジ系を吹き
つける。
❹ Spray yellow/orange system paints over the shops, passages
and arcade facade at the RH side.

❺最後に，人物と中央の植栽を着色して完成となる。
❺ Finally, color the incidental humans and greenery at the
center of the perspective.

用具の説明

短時間でキャンソンボードに仕上げるためには，大きなパ
レット（プラスチック板自家製）に薄くのばした不透明水彩絵具
を中心に用いている。広い面積を塗り込むときは経済的な
ポスターカラーを用い，濃い塗り込みと精密な作業部分は
密度の細かいデザインガッシュなどを用いている。

具体的には，以下のように様々な用途に応じて使い分けて
いる。
* 広い面積を塗り込む場合＝ポスターカラーを薄くのばし
　たり，濃くねったりして用いる
* やや細かい部分や溝さし定規とガラス棒で細い線を引
　く場合＝デザインガッシュ。一段と粒子が細かい
* 微妙な色を表現したい場合＝ホルベイン水彩絵具（透
　明・不透明）。グリーン系の色などを頻繁に使う。種類
　は豊富にある
* 固形タイプでのびがよい絵具＝ペリカン水彩絵具（不透
　明）。色質が鮮明で塗りむらをつくらない長所がある
* 色が豊富で密度粒子の細かい絵具＝ニュートン水彩絵
　具。鮮やかな色調が最高である

Painting tools and materials

To draw perspectives on a Canson board in a short
period, use mainly opaque watercolor paints that
can be thinly spread over extra-large plastic pal-
lets (that you manufacture yourself). It is recommendable to use modestly priced poster colors for coloring
the large portions of the painting, while design
gouache of fine density is better for heavy coloring
in areas of the painting that require precise detail.
The use of the painting materials should vary with
the method of application. Here are some general
guidelines for selecting and using painting media.
* When coloring a vast area: thinly spread poster
  colors over the areas that need to be colored.
  Thoroughly knead any thick, congealed portions of paint.
* When drawing fine lines with a groove scale and
  a glass rod: use design gouache, or a finer
  particle paint.
* When expressing subtle colors: use Holbein
  watercolors (Transparent/opaque). Use green-
  based colors liberally. A variety of colors are
  available.
* Solid type color paints with good stretching
  ability: use opaque Pelican watercolors. They
  have the advantages of producing a clear color
  quality and rendering in uniform colors.
* Color paints with fine density and particles in
  various colors: Newton watercolors. Paints with
  a clear color tone are best.

無人搬送立体地下駐車場計画

繁華街の地下に設置する大型地下駐車場計画

Underground multistoried parking lot with unmanned car guided system

Large underground parking lot built under shopping quarters

表現チェックポイント

立体地下駐車システムを説明するために俯瞰図で表現した。また，地中を断面にして，収納された車の様子がわかるように工夫している。地上の街並みは図面がなく，描き手の理想としてつくり上げたもの。このようなスケッチは躍動する市街の表現，そして人や車を数多く描くことが要求される。

設計コンセプトポイント

クライアントからの依頼内容と目的は，これから全国展開されていく独自な開発システム（立体駐車場）を街中に設けたときの完成予想図を作成することである。街の中心地であれば人の賑わい，道路を走る車，バスなどの描写，あるいは最寄りの駅や地下鉄駅ターミナルへのアクセス連絡道などの素材は，当然描くことになる。衰退していく街ではなく，いま以上に繁栄している街並みの景観を具体的に表現することが要求される。

Check point for mode of expression

A birds-eye-view mode of expression was utilized to present this multistory underground parking system. The underground section is drawn to show how the cars are being parked. Since no drawing of the shopping quarters above the ground was provided, the illustrator has drawn his own idealized conception of the shopping quarters. When drawing this type of sketch, it is necessary to draw as many people and cars as possible to give the streets a lively atmosphere.

Main point of design concept

The purpose of the perspective requested by the client was to present an as-built drawing of a newly developed unique type of parking lot system to be located in underground cities throughout the nation. Since the area portrayed is the center of a city, it is naturally necessary to draw many people, cars and buses, stations, concourses to the subway station, etc. It is also necessary to concretely convey the idea that the streets are part of a city which is expected to expand and prosper in the future, instead one that is going into decline.

クライアント:株式会社日立造船パーキングシステム事業部
サイズ:420mm×680mm
Client:Hitachi Zosen Parking System Co., Ltd.
Size:420mm×680mm

クライアント:株式会社日立造船パーキングシステム事業部
サイズ:420mm×680mm
Client:Hitachi Zosen Parking System Co., Ltd.
Size:420mm×680mm

❶キャンソンボードに構図線画をトレースダウンする。キャンソンボードは多少の消しゴム作業にたえる強さがあるので, 時間が緊迫しているときはキャンソンボードに直接描写作業を行うとよい。
❶ Trace down the line drawing of composition on the Canson board. Since the Canson board is durable and images drawn on Canson board can be quickly erased with a rubber eraser, it is recommended to draw the perspective directly on a Canson board when quick perspective preparation is required.

❷本番。線描画として完成させる。
❷ Finish the line drawing.

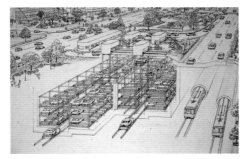

❸塗りむらを出したくないため, 建造物などのガラス部分はエアブラシでスカイブルーやウルトラマリンライトなどを使用。
❸ To avoid non-uniform painting, use sky blue or light ultra marine colors for the glazed portion of the building, and paint them using an airbrush.

❹地中を思わせる部分を，濃茶色で着色する。あまり強くなりすぎてインパクトを与えないこと。

❹ Any portion expressing the underground should be colored dark brown. Avoid placing too many highlights on an area to give impact.

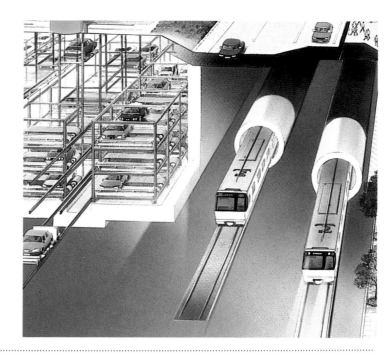

❺市街地の歩道，人物，植物などを着色する。

❺ Color the pedestrian road, incidental humans and plants of the city.

❻一番難しい乗用車の着色作業で完成。この仕事では，完成画は2案つくられた。

❻ To finish the perspective, color the cars. Cars are considered to be one of the most difficult elements in perspective drawings. In this case, two alternative perspectives have been prepared.

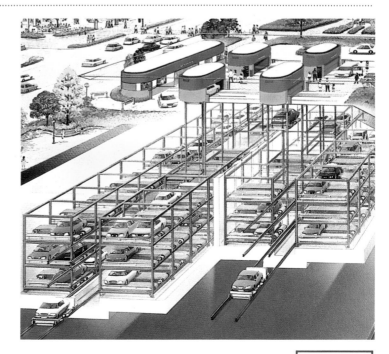

バイオテクノロジー都市計画
（株式会社上田篤都市建築研究所）

広範囲の表現が必要なため高い位置からの鳥瞰で描いた。
イメージプレゼンテーションの段階なので，
細かい部分は単純に表している。

Biotechnology City Planning
(Ueda Atsushi Urban Desgin Reseach Institute)

Since it was necessary to present a vast area, the
perspective was drawn from a higher position with a
birds-eye view. Since the perspective was intended for
image presentation, the details were expressed simply.

大阪湾人工島計画
（大阪市港湾局）

同じ鳥瞰でも低い位置からみた鳥瞰パース。海の上の
未来計画なので，海は青く，遠大な空には通常パースでは
あまり描く機会のない入道雲や海鳥などもおおらかに描き上げた。

Artificial Island Project in Osaka Bay
（Osaka Prefectural Government Port and Harbor Bureau）

This is also a birds-eye view perspective, but it was
drawn from a relatively low position. Since the project
is a future off-shore project, the sea was colored blue
and gigantic columns of clouds and seagulls, elements
which are rarely drawn in perspectives, were featured
to give the scene a sense of immensity.

工場跡地再利用計画
（株式会社上田篤都市建築研究所）

計画のレイアウトがシンメトリックなので，中央正面に位置しての
鳥瞰画で表現した。これもイメージプレゼンテーションの
段階なので，精密描写をさけて仕上げている。

Re-utilization plan of a plant site
(Ueda Atsushi Urban Desgin Reseach Institute)

Since the layout of the plant site is symmetrical, the
perspective was drawn in a birds-eye-view as seen
from the main gate. As this perspective also had to be
used for image presentation, precise details were
eliminated.

堺市都市緑化センター
（株式会社坂倉建築研究所）

広範囲で，しかも複雑な内容の場合は，ペンで
細部まで仕上げ彩色するといい。
広い敷地に温室，庭園見本園など花や緑が多くある場合には，
日頃の植物に対する勉強の成果が表れる。

Sakai City Greenery Center
(Sakakura Architectural Design & Research Institute)

When expressing complicated objects in a vast area, it
is effective to color the objects after drawing in their
details with a pen. When drawing the flowers in the
huge greenhouse and greenery in the garden displays,
any experience that you have accumulated in the daily
study of drawing plants would be useful.

第 3 章 ｜ 商 業 施 設

Chapter 3 ｜ Commercial facilities

ショッピングセンターの中央プラザ

明るい日差しと草花に囲まれた開放感あふれる休憩エリアの演出

Central plaza of shopping mall

Dramatic presentation of open rest area full of ample sunlight and flowers

表現チェックポイント

この作品は，巨大なガラス張りの吹き抜けを設け，そこに植物を配した室内小庭園のような憩いのオアシスを説明するスケッチである。大きなスペースをパブリックエリアにすることで，左右に展開するスーパーストアーゾーンや専門ファッションストアゾーンが要所となるような計画意図を提示している。ペン線描画と淡彩着色で簡単に表現はできるが，絵全体のインパクトを考えるとき，濃度のある不透明絵具で十分に塗り込み，ペン線を無視するように塗りつぶしてしまい，ボリュームのある造形をみせようとする。

設計コンセプトポイント

依頼内容から，このスケッチの構図は一点透視でフロアーの中心に立ち，臨場感が迫ってくるように一歩二歩踏み込んでとらえてみた。絵の中に立つ左右に連立する丸形の柱は，そのまま描くと向こうが見えなくなるので，下半分を透明にして専門店内部の雰囲気を表現している。

Check point for mode of expression

This sketch was used to present a room with a huge glazed well-hole with an arrangement of plants like a small garden and functions as an oasis in the middle of a rest area. The sketch presents the intention of the super store zone and specialty fashion shop zone project, and conveys the major theme of the project, i.e., utilizing the huge space as a public space. Though it is possible to express the sketch with a simple line drawing combined with light colors, efforts were made to present the voluminous objects by painting heavy opaque colors with sufficient force to make a strong impact on the viewers.

Main point of design concept

In order to meet the requirements stipulated by the client, this sketch was composed utilizing the one-point vanishing point method from a position in the center of the floor, and closer to the objects to emphasize realistic rendering of the spot. If the cylindrical columns standing on both sides of rest area were drawn as they really are, the objects behind the columns could not be seen. Therefore, the lower halves of the columns were rendered transparently so that the atmosphere of the specialty shops could be presented.

サイズ：380mm×630mm
Size：380mm×630mm

❶最初にペン線描画として完成させる。その後，マスキング液で塗りたくない部分をふさぐ。
❶ Draw the line drawing. Use masking liquid to cover the areas of the painting that should not be painted at this stage.

❷次に，遠景の売場などの細かい部分を先に着色する。
❷ Next, color the detailed portions such as the sales counters in the distance.

❸天井部分，建物壁面，下部天井部分，床全体の調子をみながら着色。
❸ Color the ceiling, wall, drop ceiling and floor, considering the total balance of tone.

❹はじめにふせていたマスキング部分を，専用のラバーゴムでこすり取る。人物，マネキン，商品などの細部に着色を進める。

❹ Scrub off the masking liquid applied earlier with a special rubber tool, and color the details of the incidental humans, mannequins, commercial goods, etc.

❺植物や人物などの点景を着色する。

❺ Color the incidental items such as plants and people.

❻植物や人物などの仕上げを最後にして，色彩のコントロールをする。これは，作品の完成度を左右するテクニックでもある。

❻ In the final stage, color the plants and people, and adjust the overall tone of the colors. The degree of completion reached in the perspective depends on this technique, so it is very important.

商業ビルの外周の環境整備計画

ヤング対象の飲食エリアの演出

Improvement plan for the environment surrounding commercial buildings

Development of restaurants for the younger generation

表現チェックポイント

カフェレストランを主体に，その周辺の環境を描く。カフェ店内と屋外が一体化した設計意図を表現するため，軽いタッチの水彩画風なスケッチとして仕上げた。左端の奥にモールを描くことで，その雰囲気がわかる。ポイントは人物の配置とその動，静，そして川と植物が自然感と空間の余裕をつくり上げていること。

設計コンセプトポイント

プロムナードには自然石を敷き，人口の小川と植物に囲まれた景観を表現するように努めた。2階のレストランなど，レトロ調で若者の街を象徴するようなアメリカンナイズされた完成予想図を水彩画タッチで仕上げた。

サイズ：430mm×700mm
Size：430mm×700mm

❶最初にペン線描画として，完全に絵にしてしまう。
❶ First, complete the line drawing.

Check point for mode of expression

This perspective presents mainly cafe restaurants and the surrounding environment. To express the design objectives of the integrated interiors and exterior portions of the indoor and outdoor areas of the restaurants, a light sketchy touch resembling watercolor painting was selected. The atmosphere can be felt by the depiction of the shopping mall in the long distance at the LH side of the picture. The main points are the arrangement of incidental humans and their dynamic and static movements, the creation of a natural feeling, and sufficient space to accommodate the river and plants.

Main point of design concept

By drawing the natural stones over the promenade, efforts were made to express the landscape full of people and the artificial brook. The perspective depicts the Americanized and retro style of the restaurants on the second floor, denoting that it is a town for the younger generation, and is painted with a sketchy touch resembling watercolor.

❷ブルー系の部分をエアブラシ（手塗りでもよいが，より美しいシャープさを出すために）で着色。床の石張り部分を彩色し，明暗をつける。この時点では，石材などの材質の描き方は未完成にしておく。
❷ Color the area containing blue hues using an airbrush (although, manual painting is allowed, the use of an airbrush is much better to give a sharpness to the painting). Color the stone-paved floor portion and finish the shaded and bright portions. Do not draw the texture of the stones used for pavement at this stage.

❸細かい窓サッシュの塗り込みは，溝尺（ガラス棒ですべらせる）で素早く仕上げる。
❸ Coloring of details of window sashes should be finished quickly using a groove scale (sliding the glass rod).

❹絵全体のバランス，色調をよくみながら人物の服装の色，植物の葉の色などカラーコントロールを考えて調整しながら着色する。
❹ Color the clothes of incidental humans and the leaves, adjusting the overall color tone and color balance.

中央空間のあるショッピングセンター計画

中央噴水をシンボルとした中庭の憩いの場

Plan of shopping mall with a wide plaza at its center

A patio rest area with a fountain constructed at its center

表現チェックポイント

中庭から正面奥にある百貨店との関連を説明するため構図を決め，この位置から描くことにした。噴水で戯れる子供たちの動きを中心に，左右に専門店や飲食店，2，3階にレストランを配置し，楽しいタッチで表現してクライアント側へのアピールを効果的にする。描写に際しては，植栽計画図面などイメージ段階では準備されていないので，描き手のほうで任意にまかせられての仕上げとなる。

設計コンセプトポイント

計画グループ（依頼者）に対する心がまえと対応で，どのようなタッチのプレゼンテーションスケッチにするか意思の疎通を図っておかないと，情熱のこもった仕上がりの作品でも，依頼者側にまったく歓迎されない場合が生ずる。そうなればクライアント側との打ち合わせ本番に，提示する気力もなくなってしまうだろう。

サイズ：410mm×723mm
Size：410mm×723mm

❶中央に噴水を配置するように構図を決めて，キャンソンボードに清書する。
❶ Decide the composition in which the fountain is arranged at the center of the perspective and transcribe it on the Canson board.

Check point for mode of expression

This composition was selected to express the relationship between the department store located in the innermost center of the scene and the patio. The composition, which depicts specialty shops on both sides of the patio and restaurants on the second and third floors, centers on the children playing around the fountain. The children are drawn with a pleasant touch, which was effective in giving the client an impression of the perspective's presentation effect. Since there were no design drawings of the plantation plan, etc., at the image creation stage of the perspective, these elements were left to the illustrator.

Main point of design concept

Unless the perspective is presented with a touch that has been approved by both the project group (client) and the illustrator, even greatly labored work may not necessarily be accepted by the client

❷人物をマスキング液でふせて，その他の着色がスムースにできるようにしてから，空，右の建物のガラス部分，中央遠くのアトリウムなどを着色する。
❷ Cover the incidental humans with masking liquid so that coloring can be smoothly applied. Color the sky, the glass on the RH side of the building, and the atrium in the distance.

❸噴水の水溜まりの微妙な表現を描き込む。
❸ Delineate the delicate form of the water pouring from the fountain.

❹右側の3，4階の飲食店の雰囲気を表現する。専門店内の色調は濃い色にする。個人差はあるが，セピア，バウントセンナーやサップグリーンなどを混合したダークな色で調子を整えるといいだろう。
❹ Express the atmosphere of the restaurants on the third and fourth floors. Choose darker colors for the specialty shops. Condition the picture using darker colors mixed with sepia, burnt sienna, or sap green.

ターミナルビルのショッピングモール

旅行者，送迎者のためのショッピング＆飲食ゾーン

Shopping mall at the terminal building

Shopping center and restaurants for travelers and those who come to welcome them or see them off

表現チェックポイント

通路中央に人物を立たせる構図を取ると，説明しやすくなる。これで左右の店の業種，業態など一目でわかるだろう。また，店内商品ディスプレーと飲食中の人々を描くことで，絵に生きた感じがでてくる。そのための描き込み努力をすること。直線部分は薄手の三角定規を用い，ロットリングペン（0.15mm）にブラックとこげ茶をプラスしたロットリングインクで描いていく。キャンソンボード本番で失敗はしないのが望ましいが，もし失敗したら着色時にポスターカラーで濃く塗りつぶして修正する。

設計コンセプトポイント

仕事を受ける際の心がまえとして，まず依頼者側のスケッチパースの仕上がりの期待感と表現のポイントを十分に聞くこと。そして，鉛筆線構図ができたところでもう一度打ち合わせを行うといいだろう。

サイズ:365mm×600mm
Size:365mm×600mm

Check point for mode of expression

If you choose a composition in which incidental people are standing in the middle of the passage, the perspective becomes more explanatory. This can provide information about the types of shops and businesses lined up along both sides of the passage. Drawing the shop displays in the shops and people in the restaurants gives the painting more vividness. Thus, some efforts are necessary to properly draw the incidental humans in the painting. Use a thin triangle scale, rottling pen (0.15mm) and black or dark brown rottling ink for drawing the straight lines. When using the Canson board, it is better not to make any mistakes in the painting. If you do make a mistake, however, use the poster colors to touch up the failed portions on the Canson board.

Main point of design concept

When you receive a request for a rendering, consult with the client about what he expects in the rendering, and what his major points are. Make a rough sketch of the composition in pencil, and show it to the client for additional discussion and guidance.

❶構図が決まって定着したら（キャンソンボード使用）鉛筆描写にはいる。専門店内部のファッションや飲食店，喫茶店内の人物の準備として割りつけをする。
❶ Once the composition was decided, start drawing with a pencil using a Canson board, and then decide the allocation of display inside the specialty shops and people in the restaurants.

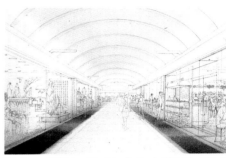

❷本番。ペン線描写をロットリングペン（0.15mm）ではじめる。次に，彩色準備にかかり，マスキングフイルムを絵全体に貼りつける。着色したい部分をカットナイフでカットする。天井，床，左右の専門店の順で着色していく。
❷ Next, start the line drawing with a rottling pen (0.15mm). Using masking film, cover the portions which are not to be painted, and then apply color. Repeat this step for coloring the ceiling, the floor, and then the specialty shops, using a knife to remove the masking film from the areas to be colored each time.

❸次に移る場合には，着色した部分をふたたびはずして，フイルムをもとの場所に貼る。
❸ Prior to moving on to the next step, cover the painted areas once more with the masking film.

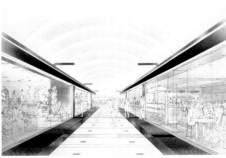

❹左右の専門店の商品と人物の色を濃くしていく。全体の色の調子をもう一度見て，初心からかけ離れた絵になっていないか，再チェックをする。
❹ Add colors to the specialty shops and the incidental humans to finalize the coloring of these elements. Review the entire color tone and balance again to ensure that the rendering has not deviated from its purpose.

ファッションビル

感覚産業が集約するファッションビル

Fashion building

Fashion building occupied by fashion business enterprises

表現チェックポイント

ファッション産業を主とする業態が一目でわかるような外観画を表現するため，いままでのパースに一味変化をつけて若者の動きを多く描き，完成後の繁華を促すような雰囲気を発散させる作風で仕上げた。力強さも必要なため，不透明水彩絵具も多用し，ペン線がつぶれるくらいに塗り込んでみた。

設計コンセプトポイント

クライアントとの打ち合わせ時に，商業ビルの運営は感覚産業といわれるセンスが商品であることを確認し，その際にクライアントとコンセプトをどこまで表現できるかをディスカッションした。

Check point for mode of expression

To draw the exterior of the building so that it could be easily identified as a fashion building, some efforts were made to draw perspective a bit differently from more conventional perspectives of fashion buildings. This was done by adding more movement of young people, and expressing the hustling and bustling atmosphere of the site. Since a vigorous feeling was required in the rendering, opaque watercolors were used to cover up the base line drawing.

Main point of design concept

Discussion with the client confirmed that the objective "sense" of the perspective was the merchandise to be sold by the management of the commercial "sense industry" building. At the same time, how far the concept should be expressed in the rendering was also discussed.

クライアント:株式会社布谷
サイズ:440mm×725mm
Client:Nunotani Co., Ltd.
Size:440mm×725mm

❶構図が定着したらキャンソンボードに本清書する。ロットリング・ドローイングインク（セピア，黒0.15mm）を使用。

❶ Once the composition is decided, transcribe it on the Canson board. Use the rottling pens (0.15mm) and ink (sepia and black).

❷マスキングフイルムで全体をふせる。

❷ Cover the entire drawing with the masking film.

❸着色したい部分をカットナイフでカットし，彩色着色にはいる。

❸ Remove the portions of the painting where the coloring is necessary with a knife and start coloring.

❹黒の着色は，エアブラシのほうがきれいに彩色できる。どうしてもよどみが生じてしまう。
❹ Use an airbrush to apply the black ink, since it can produce a clear coloring. Manual painting cannot eliminate the stagnation of color paint.

❺建造物の左右や床の色で全体の調子を見ながらカラーコントロールに気を配り，人物などでフィニッシュする。
❺ Finish the perspective by drawing the incidental humans, adjusting the overall color tone of the picture including the areas on both sides of the building and floor.

商業施設環境空間の重要性

大型店，商業施設，ショッピングセンターなどクライアントである企業は，なによりもユーザーへのサービス意識が強い。ユーザーへのサービスのために莫大な資本を投入する建設物は，単なる商業施設ではなく，より多くの人に知ってもらいたい情報の発信基地であり，コミュニケーションとネットワークの広がりに期待がかかる。そして当然のごとく，その計画が成功して資金の回収をし，やがて利益を生まなければならない。

現在のファッション業界は，単なる服飾産業ではない。またスポーツ用品業などもスポーツ衣料やスポーツ用品をつくって売るという考え方を有してはいない。それらの商品を販売する百貨店や大型ショッピングセンターなどの意識は，すべて感覚産業という認識をしている。このことを考えると，パースというデザイン設計や計画意図が，クライアントからユーザーに伝達する媒体としての役目を果たさなければならないので，責任は非常に重要である。クライアント，クリエイティブグループ，パースデザイナー，すべての関係者たちの真剣勝負なのである。

Importance of creating the environmental space for the commercial facilities

The enterprises that employ perspective designers, i.e., large shops, commercial facilities and shopping centers, have a strong user-oriented service consciousness. These clients invest so much money in their commercial buildings not only for the sake of user service; they are not only the mere commercial facilities, they also function as data sending stations which the clients hope to expand into communication networks. Accordingly, it is only natural that the clients expect to have their investments returned sooner or later when their projects succeed.

The contemporary fashion industry is not merely an apparel industry, just as the sporting goods manufacturing industry does not limit its business strictly to the simple activities of manufacturing and selling sporting apparel and goods. Department stores and large shopping malls consider their businesses as part of the "feeling industry." Since perspective sketches should function as a

means to convey the client's design concepts and intentions to the users, the role of perspective designers is quite important. This is an arena of battle for the clients, the creative team, the perspective designers and the people in related fields.

商店街アーケード計画

新興商店街に対抗する旧商店街通りの復興

Arcade construction plan for the shopping mall

Restoration of old shopping mall to compete with a new shopping area

表現チェックポイント

完成後の賑やかさと繁栄の予想を商店主たちにアピールするため，臨場感を強く印象づける人々の動きと各店舗の雰囲気描写に気をつけた。モールに見えるサインボードや電話ボックスなど，すべて依頼者からの提示はなく，描き手のほうでセンスあるデザインを選択し描き込んでいく。人物やマネキン人形などのプロポーションには特に注意する。

設計コンセプトポイント

新興都市の発展に対抗して旧商店街新興のため新設するアーケードが，明るくモダンなショッピングモールに変貌する期待感が大きなポイントになることに留意して描く。

Check point for mode of expression

To give the owners of the shops in the area an impression of the thriving and prosperous growth that could be expected in the area after the completion of restoration, extra care was taken in drawing the movement of people, and in creating a strongly realistic atmosphere——an atmosphere similar to what one would experience when actually standing in the real mall. Though they were not requested, objects such as advertising boards and telephone booths were drawn at the discretion of the illustrator, based on his sense of rendering. Special care was also be taken in the proportions of the incidental humans and mannequins in the drawing.

Main point of design concept

The most important point in this perspective is to help the client visualize the arcade of the restored shopping mall, which will compete with a new shopping mall, and to visualize how it will become modern and bright.

サイズ:400mm×550mm
Size:400mm×550mm

❶キャンソンボードに鉛筆線描きをする。納得いくまでデッサンと構図を練る。鉛筆線の上からペン線描画として完成させる。もちろん人物，植物，電話ボックスもすべて描写，清書を終える。

❶ Draw on the Canson board with a pencil. Work on your own ideas for the sketch and composition until you are satisfied. Finish a pen line drawing overlapping the pencil lines. Before finishing the painting, make sure to include incidental items such as people, plants and telephone booths.

❷マスキングフイルムを全面に貼りつけ，エアブラシで彩色したいところを，順々にはずして着色する。

❷ Apply masking film over the entire painting, and remove the areas in the painting that you wish to paint at each stage.

❸アーケードのスチールサッシュ部分を着色する。手塗りよりエアブラシのほうがきれいに仕上る。

❸ Color the aluminum sashes in the arcade. Cleaner and more beautiful coloring can be expected if you use an airbrush.

❹店舗壁面部分，床，道路部分をひと通りエアブラシで着色したあと，手塗りで第2段階，第3段階のコントラストのアクセントをつけていく。

❹ After coloring the wall, floor and passage in the shops with an airbrush, accent the perspective in the second and third stages of manual painting by adjusting the color contrast.

❺直線的な塗り込みの部分は溝さし定規とガラス棒で着色する。最後に，人物などは色調をコントロールしながら，また，作品全体の調子により植物などの色調はそのつど変化させてフィニッシュとなる。

❺ Color the straight lines using a groove scale and glass rod. Finally, paint in the incidental people and plants. Adjust the color tone, and change the coloring of the people and plants according to the total color balance with the rest of the picture.

アーケード・リニューアル計画
青空が見える開閉天井を設けたモダンな商店街

Renewal project of arcade
Modern shopping mall featuring an opening and closing type arc
with a ceiling that reveals the sky

❶円，曲線が多い線描作業。コンパス，ペン取りつけ用コンパス，雲形定規など使いこなしながら描いていく。
❶ Line drawing of many circles and curved lines. Use the compass, compass for attaching the pen, curved rule, etc., in a correct manner.

0 6 5

表現チェックポイント

通路中央から奥行き方向でパースを設定する。個人商店は，既存店よりもモダンな店舗になるように描く。直線と曲線の作業が多いので，前述したペン専用コンパスで天井アーケードのアールを描く。人物もバラエティに富ませ，賑やかにする。

設計コンセプトポイント

商店街の繁栄を切望しているクライアント（商店街）に迎合される雰囲気をもった画風に描き上げるように，依頼者と描写表現のうえで多少妥協しながらも描く。

Check point for mode of expression

Render the perspective expressing the central passage of the shopping mall in its longitudinal direction. Draw the specialty shops so that they look more modern than the existing conventional shops. Since you have to draw many straight and curved lines, use the special compass for the drawing pen when drawing the curved area of the ceiling in the arcade. Draw a variety of incidental people in a lively manner.

Main point of design concept

To a certain degree, compromise with the client in the drawing or expression of the perspective so that the final outcome will have an atmosphere that the clients approve of. It is very important to the client that the prosperous atmosphere of the shopping mall is effectively conveyed in the drawing.

❷直線は薄手の三角定規の薄手を使用すると，うまく描ける。
❷ Use the thin triangle scale to draw straight lines correctly.

❸この場合商店の建物は添景となるが，適当な変化と活動する人物などの遠近感を考えながら着色していく。
❸ In this perspective, the buildings of the shopping mall and activity within them become incidental items. But when drawing incidental items, including the people working in the shops, etc., and incorporate a variety of colors and form.

❹全体の色のトーンを考えながら仕上げる。
❹ Finish up the perspective paying close attention the overall balance of tone.

クライアント:株式会社日米アートム・アーケード事業部
サイズ:430mm×300mm
Client:Nichibei-Artm Arcade Business Dept.
Size:430mm×300mm

ホテル内の高級レストラン

ホテル内ラウンジのような欧州風レストランルーム

A deluxe restaurant in a hotel

European-type restaurant that resembles the lounge of a hotel

表現チェックポイント

構図として，入口付近からルーム奥部全景をのぞむ位置からのパーススケッチにする。キャンソンボード上にやわらかい鉛筆を用い軽いタッチでデッサンし，定着させてからペン線描画として完成させる。ペンで完成させることが，絵に対する正確さと判断，決断の早さにつながる。絵全体のインパクトを強めるため，厚塗りになってもいい。淡彩仕上げだけにとどまらず，どんどん不透明絵具も使用する。

設計コンセプトポイント

依頼内容には，楽しい色調と奥ガラス窓からの逆光線の雰囲気や会食中のカラフルな服装の人物たち，ゴージャスなスペースのゆとりを見せたいという意見があり，それらに重点をおき作画した。

Check point for mode of expression

Draw a perspective sketch of the overall view of the restaurant. Include the remote distance of the interior, depicting the way the restaurant might look when viewed from the vicinity of its entrance. Lightly sketch the perspective on a Canson board with a soft pencil, and after the sketch has been completed, finish it as a pen line drawing. By finishing the perspective with a pen, a quicker and more precise presentation of the scene can be made. If executed skillfully, heavy painting might be acceptable as a way to enhance the impact of the entire perspective. Try to use opaque colors as much as possible instead of finishing the perspective lightly.

Main point of design concept

The client requested that the backlighting from the window panes in the distance create a pleasant, nicely colored atmosphere, and that the luxurious space of the restaurant be included, complete with guests in fashionable, colorful wardrobes. Therefore, emphasis was placed on expressing these features in the perspective.

クライアント:株式会社AAA総合設計
サイズ:340mm×620mm
Client: AAA Sogo Design Co,. Ltd.
Size:340mm×620mm

❶素早く仕上げるためにペン画として完成させる。着色彩色しなくても、その雰囲気が表現されるようにする。

❶ Draw the perspective as a line drawing so that it can be quickly finished. The drawing can express the atmosphere of restaurant without coloring.

❹同様に、床面も第1段階の平筆で彩色していく。

❹ Similarly, color the floor with a flat brush in the first stage of painting.

❷天井と床面が最初の作業となるため、その他の部分をマスキング液でふせてしまう。面積を広くふさぐ場合は、マスキングフイルムを使用する。

❷ Since the ceiling and the floor should be drawn first, the other areas must be masked with the masking liquid. When it is necessary to mask wider areas, use the masking film.

❺天井のポイントである彩色を終わらせる。

❺ Finish the coloring of the floor, one of the important points in the perspective.

❸天井から素早く広幅な筆（平筆）で、左右に塗り込んでいく。

❸ Color the ceiling quickly with a wide (flat) brush, applying colors on both the RH and LH sides.

❻床のチェック模様は、基本色となるベージュで調子を出す。

❻ When drawing the checked pattern on the floor, adjust the tone using a beige variation of the basic color.

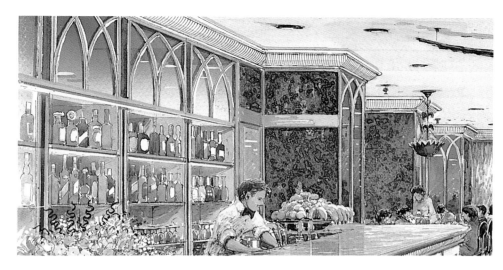

❼室内ミラー貼り部分やガラス材のところは、エアブラシのほうが美しくできる。

❼ To finish the perspective with a beautiful touch, use an airbrush when drawing the portion of the room with the built-in mirror and glass material.

❽個性の強い壁面クロスは、水分の多い筆ではじめにたっぷりと色を塗り、濡れているあいだに食塩を振りかける。乾くと複雑な模様が現れる。

❽ When drawing the unique wall cloth, begin by applying the color amply with a very wet brush, and then sprinkle table salt over the painting while it is still wet. This will create a complicated and interesting pattern when the painting dries.

❾フリーハンドによる彩色着色をすませておく。

❾ Before applying the final colors, all of the freehand coloring should be finished.

ショッピングセンター・エントランス

正面入口のドアデザインの検討スケッチ

Entrance to a shopping mall

Sketch for reviewing of the entrance door design

表現チェックポイント

正面から館内奥行き感を表現すると，より空間と距離がわかる。人物の配置は，入口付近から館内まで描き，店内の様子もガラスケースの陳列や応対中の店員も忘れずに描く。そして全体的に屋外と館内を比べて，館内のほうが暗くなるように描く。

設計コンセプトポイント

依頼を受けてからの心がまえとして，なぜこのパースが必要かという疑問をもちながら打ち合わせに対応すると，早く構図が決まる。正面入口のデザイン検討を確実にしておけば，どのような光景の作品として仕上げるべきかが決まってくる。

Check point for mode of expression

If the distance from the main entrance to the remote portion of the shopping mall is drawn, the space and distance can be more clearly expressed. When drawing in the incidental items and people near the entrance to the shopping mall, do not forget to include the shop clerks attending their customers and the displays and showcases in the stores. Generally, make the inside of the shopping mall darker than the outside of the mall.

Main point of design concept

If you continue to investigate the purpose of this perspective during your discussion with the client, the idea and the composition will take shape quickly. As long as the entrance design has been confirmed in your discussion, the idea of how the perspective should be finished comes out readily.

サイズ:300mm×480mm
Size:300mm×480mm

❶鉛筆で，割りつけ線画をキャンソンボードに描く。
❶ Draw the allocation line drawing on a Canson board with a pencil.

❷次に，本清書としてペン線描画を完成させる。
❷ Next, finish the line drawing with a pen.

❸マスキングフイルム貼り，カット，という手順で，天井，入口床部の着色（エアブラシ），そして館内もダークな色でエアブラシ着彩。
❸ Prepare by applying the masking film. Color the floor of the entrance and the ceiling with an airbrush, and then cut away the masking film. Color the interior of the shopping mall in a dark color with the airbrush.

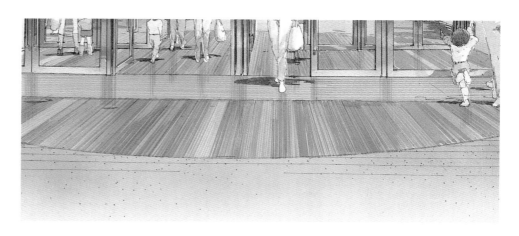

❹入口から内部にわたる木調デザインの床材の着彩。溝さし定規とガラス棒を利用する。

❹ Color the portions of the floor that are designed to have a wooden grain finish. These portions are near the entrance of the shopping mall, and in the interior. Use the groove scale and the glass rod.

❺館内の色をもう少し濃く塗る。

❺ Lightly apply additional colors over the colors already in the interior of the shopping mall.

❻最後に，このスケッチで一番ポイントとなる鏡面仕上げ（ステンレス鏡面仕上げ）の表現の段階的な色彩による着色作業をすませ，大きな人物を淡彩な調子でまとめる。

❻ Finally, color the most important points in the perspective. Use a gradual, step-by-step coloring method for the stainless steel mirror finish, and then adjust the coloration of the large human subjects with a light touch.

商業ビル

中央大吹き抜けの空間をもつハイファッションビル

Commercial building

High fashion building with a large well-hole at its center

❷2F、3Fの天井部分のみカットナイフで切りはずし、エアブラシで吹きつけ
着彩をする。同様に、専門店部分の奥行き感を着彩する。ディスプレーや
カウンターケースなどは、そのあとに手書きで塗り込みをする。
❷ Use a knife to cut away the masking film covering the ceilings
of the second and third floors, and spray colors over these areas
with an airbrush. Similarly, use color to give depth to the specialty shops. Next, the displays and counter cases should be
colored manually.

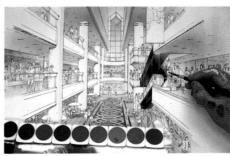

❸専門店内の光景を描く。1F床のデザイン模様を描いたのち、人物を着彩
する。服装や天井吊りデザイン幕の色調で、絵全体のバランスをコントロー
ルする。
❸ Draw the scene of specialty shops. After drawing the design
pattern on the 1st floor, color the people in the scene. Condition
the overall tone of the perspective by balancing the colors of the
clothes of the people and the banner dangling from the ceiling.

❹完成。
❹ Completion of perspective.

表現チェックポイント

空間の広さを表現する構図にするため、2Fに水平線をとる。館内の奥行き感と3,
4Fの上部採光窓の特徴、そして1F床面の個性あるデザインなどの表情と感性が十
分に伝わるスケッチになるよう気をつけた。

設計コンセプトポイント

建造物の説明はもとより、商品が陳列され、人が入った完成後の賑わいを臨場感あ
ふれる雰囲気に仕上げることに留意する。ポイントは、人の動と静の表現の変化に
気をつけること。棒立ちの人物がいたり、ショップの商品が見えなかったり、あるい
は業態がつかめないと、すべてが台なしで覇気が感じられない絵になってしまう。

Check point for mode of expression

Take a horizontal line at the level of the second floor so that a composition which expresses the vastness of the space can be selected. Extra
care was exercised to convey the depth of the inside of the building, the
characteristics of the top light windows of the third and the fourth floors,
and the unique design of the first floor.

Main point of design concept

Try to draw the displays in the shops and the people shopping so that
they provide an atmosphere which makes the viewers imagine the hustle
and bustle that the high fashion shops will have after they are constructed. The point here is to give variation to the expression of the dynamic
and static movements of the people in the perspective. If only incidental
people were drawn, and no merchandise was displayed and the types of
shops could not be identified, then everything in the perspective would
be spoiled and the drawing would have no point of appeal.

サイズ:358mm×450mm
Size:358mm×450mm

大阪戎橋アーケード計画
（株式会社アパ・アソシエイツ）

アーケードのライティングテクニック効果を表現するため，
夜景で描いた。商店街の繁華の様子を前面に押し出すために，
楽しそうに歩く若者たち多く配してみた。

Osaka Ebisubashi Arcade
（APA & Associates）

A night view was selected to express the effect of a
lighting technique for the arcade. Mainly to draw the
hustling and bustling scene of the shopping mall,
groups of young people are featured walking cheerfully
in front of the shopping mall.

総合結婚式場・ホテルシェレナ

宣伝広告用のパースとして描いたもの。結婚式場の雰囲気を
出すために，あえて参列者らしき人物を手前に配置してみた。

Comprehensive Wedding Hall at Hotel Sherena

The perspective was drawn for publicity use. To
express the atmosphere of the wedding hall, people
who look like they have been invited to a party are
included in the foreground.

百貨店の1Fファッションフロア

ファッションフロアのスケッチは，当然のごとくファッションセンスが
重要視される。
人物や並んでいる商品，特にアイキャッチャーウインドーに
置かれているマネキン人形などの描き方に注意する。

Fashion floor on the ground floor of a Department store

When sketching the fashion floor, it is only natural that
a sense of fashion is necessary. Extra care should be
exercised when drawing the people and displays,
especially the mannequins standing in the eye-catching
windows.

商業ビル
（簑原建築設計事務所）

ディティールを重視して，商業ビル全体を描いてみたパース。

Commercial Building
(Minohara Architects and Design Office)

This is a perspective drawing of the entire commercial
building. Emphasis was placed on the details.

大型クルーザー船内風景

船内でのパーティーの様子を，人物を中心に優雅に描いてみた。

Interior of a large cruiser

A party scene on a cruiser. Efforts were made to draw
the incidental people with an elegant touch.

商店街アーケード
（株式会社日米アートム・アーケード事業部）

新しいアーケードが街の顔となるように，明るく華やかな雰囲気を
出すように心がけた作品。

Arcade in a shopping mall
(Nichibei-Artm Arcade Business Dept.)

Great efforts were made to express the pleasant and
gay atmosphere of the new arcade of the shopping
mall so that it would become the new landmark of the
town.

大阪心斎橋アーケード計画
（株式会社鴻池組）

歴史のある商店街なので，古風な感じを出すために
あえて色調を押さえて描いた。

Osaka Shinsai-bashi Arcade project
（Konoike-gumi Co., Ltd.）

Since this shopping mall has had a long history, efforts
were made to tone down the color to express an
antique style.

ライブハウス室内

盛り上がっている活気のあるコンサートの雰囲気を
イラスト風に仕上げた。

Interior of a music club

The atmosphere of a lively concert was expressed in an
illustrative style.

イベント広場

建造物よりも人物の動きが中心となり, 楽しい雰囲気が
伝わるように仕上げられたスケッチ。

Event plaza

Emphasis was placed on the people rather than on the
structures. This helps to convey a cheerful atmosphere
to the viewer.

自動車ショールーム
（簑原建築設計事務所）

業種の性格上，商品である車を正確に描くのがポイントと
なるため，雑誌やパンフレットなど資料を十分に準備して，
ていねいに描くことが重要である。

Showroom for automobiles
(Minohara Architects and Design Office)

One of the main objectives was to precisely draw the
automobiles displayed in the showroom. Therefore, it
was important to carefully study photographs and data
featured in magazines and pamphlets, etc.

レストラン光景

指定された建築材料をていねいに表現する。床，正面のタイル，
壁，カウンターなどサンプルを参考にして忠実に描いたスケッチ。

Scene in a restaurant

Expresses the texture of the designated construction
material. The floor, facade tiles, wall and counters in
the sketch were drawn realistically by referring to the
material samples.

第 4 章　公 共 施 設

Chapter 4｜Public facilities

学園都市文化交流センター

交流学生室，実技研修室内から学生食堂をのぞむ

Cultural exchange center in a college town

View of a cafeteria from an exchange student's room
and a study and training room.

Cultural exchange center in a college town

表現チェックポイント

シースルーの室内から連なる食堂や中庭のゆとりある空間をみせることにポイントをおき，人物の動作まで細かく描写し，イラストのように仕上げた典型的なペン画である。ビギナーには，淡彩塗りの方式をマスターするための演習が大切。

設計コンセプトポイント

依頼者の希望は，活動的な人々の姿を画面に表現することであった。仕上がったこの画風はレンダラーの表現であり，これとは逆に地味で静かな作品にする方法もある。

Check point for mode of expression

The perspective intends to show the exchange student's view of the cafeteria and spacious patio seen from the study and training room on the other side of a see-through partition. It is a typical pen drawing composition and is finished like an illustration closely delineating the movement of the people inside the cafeteria. For beginners, it is important to practice drawings for mastering light coloring technique.

Main point of design concept

The client wanted the perspective to portray people working actively in the cafeteria. This perspective shows the renderer's style of painting. It was also possible to present the work more simply and quietly.

サイズ:385mm×650mm
Size:385mm×650mm

❶構図が定着し，本清書をペン線描画として完成させる。
❶ Decide on the composition, and finish the perspective as a pen drawing.

❷はじめに色をつけたくない部分をマスキング液で塗りふせておく。
❷ Using masking film, cover the areas where coloring is not necessary in the initial stage.

❸天井面（空が見える），ガラススクリーンを着色する。
❸ Color the ceiling and the glass screen that shows the sky.

❹屋外の遠景や近景の建物の着色する。
❹ Color the near and far distance in the outdoor landscape.

❺全体の調子に照らして，大きな樹木などの配色も決める。
❺ Decide on the color of the large trees so that it harmonizes with the overall tone of the picture.

パースはプレゼンテーションにおける一手段である

設計計画案を的確に第三者に伝えるため，模型やビデオ映像，口頭説明とならんで速く仕上げるがことできるのがパースのテクニックである。一般的には，建築パースといわれている精密なレンダリング技法ではどうしても不都合な場合，あるいはまだ計画が流動的な場合に，はじめて短時間仕上げの技法であるパーススケッチが必要となってくる。

Perspectives are important for making presentations

Like models, video imaging, and verbal presentations, perspective sketches are one of the quickest and most effective ways to properly convey the intention of a design plan to a third person. In general, if a sophisticated architectural perspective is not effective to convey a design plan, or if the plan has not yet been consolidated, then it becomes necessary to employ an effective method which can be quickly executed, i.e, a perspective sketch technique.

欧州風郊外学園計画

欧州風の美しい学園キャンパスと池のある中央庭園の展開

European style suburban college town

Development of beautiful European style campus and central garden with a pond

サイズ:335mm×585mm
Size:335mm×585mm

❶用紙はキャンソンボード（白）、そこにペン線描画として完成する。
❶ Use a Canson board (white) and finish the work as a pen line drawing.

Check point for mode of expression

When planning out the composition of the sketch, make sure that the ample space between the buildings of the campus is expressed. In drawing the picture, make an effort to convey the atmosphere of a liberal and comfortable campus life.

Main point of design concept

Data and information were not provided and only verbal images were explained, so it was left to the illustrator to define the composition and choose an effective method of expressing the images. You should always keep an interest in sketches and art, and continue to practice illustration.

❷淡彩画の要領で空や正面の建物をすませ、あとは池の色調に気をつけること。
❷ Finish the sky and facade of the building with a light coloring touch. Take the tone of the pond into consideration.

❸最後は大きな木の着色。はみだし失敗の部分は不透明絵具で復元して、全体の調子を整える。
❸ Next, color the big trees. Apply opaque colors over the areas where the initial coloring needs correction, and adjust the overall color tone of the composition.

カルチャーセンター

自然に親しめる長期滞在住居ゾーン

Culture center

Nature-conscious residential for extended stays

せせらぎのある自然遊歩道を設けた贅沢な空間をポイントに描いた。人物の動きに注意し，植物の種類とその特徴を中心に仕上げた。路面など材質にとらわれずに明るく描き，歩道に沿った浅いせせらぎなどは，空色との関連を考慮して色調を決める。右手のカフェレストランはあまり調子を強くせず，軽く薄い表現でおさめ，木陰の色にも明るい日差しを感じさせる工夫をしてみた。

設計コンセプトポイント

プレゼンテーション時点では，計画グループから別段詳細な図面は提出されず，ほとんど口頭説明で作画にはいった。そのために，多くの知識をこちら側で準備して，描いていくプロセスが続く。ビジュアルなものに対する予備知識がかなり充実していないと，限られた時間での作画はうまく進まない。

Check point for mode of expression

The objective was to render the luxurious space with the natural promenade and brook. Efforts were made to emphasize the many types of trees in the scene, their many special qualities, and the movement of the people. Draw the road surface brightly without sticking to the texture of the painting material, and consider the tone of the sky when deciding the coloring for the shallow brook along the promenade. Avoid excessive highlighting of the cafe restaurant on the RH side and express it with a light and thin color touch. Efforts were made to express the shade of the trees so that the bright sunshine could be felt.

Main point of design concept

When the presentation was made, no detailed design drawing was provided, and only verbal explanation was made. Therefore, it was necessary for the illustrator to prepare and collect the necessary information for drawing. Unless the illustrator had sufficient preliminary knowledge about the visual objects, it would have been impossible to successfully draw this scene within a short period.

サイズ：350mm×650mm
Size:350mm×650mm

❶全体の構図を決め，ペン線描画として仕上げていく。
❶ Decide on the composition and finish the work as a pen line drawing.

❷空，歩道，そして小川の着色をする。この段階で植物の影も路面に描いてしまう。
❷ Color the sky, road, and brook. Put in the shading of the plants on the road at this stage.

❸遠景の建物を着色する。そしてメインである植物に取りかかる。植栽のそれぞれのグリーンが微妙に変化した色になる。
❸ Color the buildings in the distance, and then draw the main trees and plants. Make sure that the green of the plants is subtly varied from tree to tree.

❹低木のグリーンも着色する。最後に大きな木の葉をボリュームを考え，やすれた面相筆でつつくように着色していく。
❹ Color the green over the bush trees and then color the leaves of the big trees. Remember to take the volume of the leaves into consideration. Pick at the canvas with a slightly worn brush to perform coloring.

❺人物と，その足元，木陰などの明度でこの絵の全体の調子の強弱をつけ，彩色を終える。
❺ Finish the coloring by accenting the brightness of such things as the incidental people, their legs, and the shade of the trees.

短時間仕上げのための演習訓練は必須

パースデザイナーは，建築家，計画グループ，建築デザイナーなどのクリエイティブグループからの平面略図による簡単な説明を，立体空間に置き換えて，的確に設計意図や設計思想概念を把握しなくてはならない。そして，いままで集積された自分自身のデザインソースや知識を駆使し，頭の中でスケッチの構図を決めていく。

短時間作画作業になるため，その絵に必要な記憶や残像をフルに活用する。また，画面構成に重要なポイントである臨場感，そして絶対条件であるビジュアルなデッサン描写バランスはもちろん不可欠なものになる。

クリエイティブグループとは，線画（割りつけ）ができた時点で綿密な打ち合わせをする。ここで，彼らは自分たちの考え方を増幅させながら，最終チェックを画面上ですませる。これによって彩色作業へと進められていく。彩色し，いちおう感じがつかめる段階に達したら，再検討がなされる。クリエイティブグループはひと通りの作業では満足な仕上がり完成とはなかなか承知しない。そのためにパースデザイナーは，限りなく内に広がる彼らの発想のイメージの世界へあくなき追求をしていかなくてはならない。

Without practice and training it would be impossible to master the techniques to quickly finish perspective sketches.

A good perspective designer should be able to listen to an architect, project planner or architect designer briefly summarize a project plan, grasp the idea, and accurately use it to generate a three-dimensional space presentation. In deciding upon a suitable design perspective, the perspective designer should make full use of his design sources and the knowledge about design that he has accumulated.

Since the work should be completed in a short period, it is necessary for the renderer to make full use of his memories and the residual images that he can conjure in his mind. Of course, the most important challenge is to create a sense of realism from the viewpoint of the person examining the perspective, or a sense of actually being in the scene. Visual sketch presentation is also indispensable.

A detailed discussion with the creative team is imperative once the allocation of the lines has been finished. By referring to the line drawing, the creatire group can expand their image on the plan and perform a final review the ideas that they have proposed. After a final confirmation of the idea has been made, the perspective sketch can be colored. Once the coloring has been finished, the image should be reviewed again. Usually the creative team is not satisfied with what is roughly presented, but it does accept it as a final work. Therefore, the perspective designer should sometimes make an effort to search and pursue the images that are continuously being generated and expanded by the creative team.

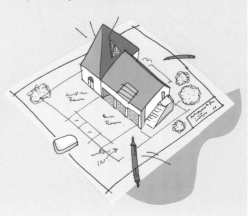

ターミナル地下街コンコース

自然採光あふれる大円形吹き抜けアトリウムをもつ地下コンコース

Underground concourse at a terminal building

**Underground concourse with a large circular well-hole atrium
allowing the entry of natural lighting**

表現チェックポイント

円形曲面などの構図に安定感がなく，作画しにくい題材が，最近多くなった。それでも画面上にたくみに描くことを考え，床面，天井面の円形リズムと吹き抜け部分のエスカレータと正面右端のファッション店ウインドーとにポイントを取った。あとは，通行中の人物や立話をしている人々の変化がある描写で全体の安定を図る。

設計コンセプトポイント

依頼に対する心がまえは，施設完成後の人々の流れや目的地への通りの素晴らしさ，将来の商業施設，繁栄の約束を物語る画風にするように気を配ること。

サイズ：322mm×610mm
Size:322mm×610mm

❶構図を決めて，本清書としてペン線描画を完成させる。
❶ Decide on the composition, and finish the perspective as a pen line drawing.

Check point for mode of expression

Of late, the number of perspective objects which have circular or curved surfaces is increasing, and this is making compositions unstable. Efforts should be made here to place a priority on the circular rhythm of the floor, ceiling, escalator in the well-hole, and fashion shop's windows at RH side of the perspective. Before stabilizing the whole picture, add variation to the picture by drawing people in the passage or talking in the street.

Main point of design concept

In presenting the perspective to the client, keep in mind that it should express the smooth flow of people moving towards the facility or destination. Emphasize the feeling that the facilities are complete, and try to create a prosperous image for the commercial components within the scene.

❷マスキングフイルムで全面をふせ，着色したい順にカットナイフでカットして着色していく。なるべく一度にガラスアトリウムを仕上げていく。天井部分も着色する。
❷ Cover the entire picture with the masking film, and cut the film over the areas to be colored in the initial stage. If possible, try to finish the glass atrium in one session. Color the ceiling portion.

❸建物壁面の着彩。石材のような材質を表す場合，タオルを小さく丸めて，叩きながらザラ目を表現する。
❸ Color the wall portion of the building. When expressing the texture of the stone, bunch up a little section of towel and express the rough touch by tapping the towel onto the canvas.

❹一番肝心な人物の彩色にはいる。最終色彩コントロールを服装の色，ウインドーディスプレーなどで決定する。このパースは，通常より色調を意識して地味に仕上げた。決まりはないので，人物の服装などカラフルにしても間違いではない。依頼者の好みで仕上げ方や表情にもそのつど変化をもたせる。
❹ Color the people, an important part of this perspective. Decide the final color control by the colors of the clothes and the window displays. This perspective has been intentionally finished using plain colors. Since there are no rules on the coloring, you can choose more colorful and gay colors for the incidental people's clothes. The finished touch depends on the client's request.

レジャー施設内の大温室

大ジャングル庭園 & カフェ休憩所のある光景

A large greenhouse in a leisure facility

A large jungle garden and a cafe

❶ペン線描画が完成したら、着彩の順序として主な植物の葉や人物などをマスキング液で塗りふせ、淡彩作業にはいる。板張りの床だけは、周囲をフイルムでふせておいて着彩するときれいにできる。

❶ Once the pen line drawing has been finished, cover the leaves of the major tropical plants and incidental people with the masking film. The wooden board flooring can be clearly painted if the areas surrounding it are covered with masking film.

表現チェックポイント

温室内の空間の広さを表現することが狙い。建物はまだ決まったものでなく、イメージの段階で天井を高くしてフレームを組み、任意の位置に植物を吊し、メインに巨大南洋植物を配置した構図にした。曲面ばかりの空間は、タッチは多少荒くても素早くペン線描画で仕上げてしまうこと。大温室のような空間では、平面となる床はあるが、曲線で囲まれた池、喫茶コーナー、蛇行する通路など表現のテクニックが要求される。天井ははるか遠く、シースルーのスチールサッシュなどは、本決まりではなくてもそれらしい表現が要求される。また、屋外の感じも含めて遠近感を出すようにする。

設計コンセプトポイント

依頼者との打ち合わせで、形よりイメージ空間中心のスケッチを期待してもらうように説明し、作画を開始した。この作品は、植物と人物が主なスケッチとなるため、日頃のデッサンや写生の演習が役立つもの。熱帯植物の参考のために、実際の温室を見学するのもいいだろう。景観は複雑でも、池、通路、喫茶室など、すべて平面で、一般スケッチの場合同様、遠近感の練習どおり表現する。思わぬペン線画の失敗部分は、不透明ガッシュやポスターカラーでつぶして仕上げていく。すんなり表現できたら、線画部、植物、人物などの彩色は透明水彩絵具、不透明水彩絵具で素早く塗る。

※塗りむらをなくす方法としては、皿の中にトリパブA液を入れると絵具の伸びがよくなる。

❷水色系の池を着彩。天井、透けてみえる空と屋外空間はブルー系で淡彩着色。この絵の主役であるグリーン系の植物と人物を着彩する。

❷ Color the pond with the blue system color. Color the ceiling, see-through sky and outdoor space with blue system color. The plants and human subjects, major objects of this perspective, should be colored with green system colors.

Check point for mode of expression

The objective of this perspective is to express the vast space in the large greenhouse. The design of the building has not been decided yet. Therefore, as the composition of the perspective, the high ceiling frame was drawn and plants were hung from the frame. The huge tropical plant was drawn as the main object. The curved surfaces in the space were quickly finished as a pen line drawing, although the touch is rather rough. When drawing the large greenhouse, it is necessary to express such elements as the pond surrounded by the curved lines, the coffee house, the winding passage, and the flat floor. The ceiling is quite high, and although the type of sash for the see-through areas has not been decided yet, the basic image of the sash should be expressed. The depth of the objects, including the outdoor landscape, should be expressed.

Main point of design concept

During the discussion between the illustrator and the client prior the first sketch, the illustrator told the client that he should expect a perspective that would center on the expression of space rather than on the actual forms themselves. As the tropical plants and human subjects are the major theme in this perspective, practice sketches of these elements would be quite helpful. To get a feel for the tropical plants, it is recommended that you visit a botanical garden or greenhouse where tropical plants are growing. Although the landscape of this perspective looks complex, the scene of the pond, passage and coffee house are all flat, and do not differ from the normal sketch. Therefore, the depth of the perspective should be expressed as it has been practiced. Portions of the pen line drawing that need to be redone can be erased by opaque gouache or poster colors. Once the objects in the perspective are smoothly drawn, quickly apply the transparent watercolors and opaque watercolors over them.

＊ To achieve uniform painting, add "tripub-A" solution to the pallet so that the colors can be spread.

❸ポイントの芭蕉の葉をもう一度印象強く仕上げる。最後に中吊りの植物や花を引き締めて着彩していく。

❸ Once again, make final touches to the leaves of the Japanese banana plant, the main point of the perspective, to make them impressive. Finally, sharply color the hung plants and flowers.

サイズ:355mm×580mm
Size:355mm×580mm

墓地整備計画
（株式会社三井建設大阪支社）

既存の建物や林に囲まれている状況を再確認するのにベストな
表現として，鳥瞰パースで描いた作品。

Tome Completion Project
(Osaka Branch of Mitsui Construction Co., Ltd.)

A birds-eye view was selected for the scene so that the
current tone of the surrounding buildings and forests
could be conveyed as effectively as possible.

学校グランド計画
（株式会社三井不動産）

この鳥瞰スケッチは周囲の自然環境を残す意味で，
あえて杉林の緑をていねいに描いてみた。

A school ground
(Mitsui Fudosan Co., Ltd.)

In this birds-eye view sketch, the cider forest was
carefully colored green to express the nature that was
to surround the school.

郊外開発計画

短時間仕上げで描かれた，広い地域にわたる鳥瞰スケッチ。

Suburb development plan

This birds-eye view sketch was prepared in a short
period to express a vast area.

ベルメゾン八ケ岳研修センター

PR用に使用されるため，あえてメルヘン風な楽しい雰囲気に
仕上げられたものである。

Bell Mason Yatsugatake Training Center

Since the perspective was intended for publicity, a
pleasant atmosphere of the style was deliberately
conveyed.

四国宇和島町文化会館計画
（株式会社設計事務所ゲンプラン）

表現の難しいコンクリート打ち放しと，全面の広いガラス部分の
表現が苦労した作品で。依頼者からの要求が不安定な
角度からの表現であっても，描き手であるわれわれには，
それをバランスよくみせるためのテクニックが必要になる。

Shikoku Uwajima Culture Hall construction plan
（GEN Plan Co., Ltd.)

Special efforts were made to express the exposed
concrete wall, a task which was inherently difficult, and
also to express the large glass wall at the facade. Even
if the client requests to have the perspective drawn
from a very difficult angle, the illustrator should satisfy
this request and put forth his best efforts to express a
well-balanced perspective.

矢田障害者会館新築工事
（株式会社贊建）

周辺環境と会館の構造のおさまりがよくわかるように，鳥瞰で
仕上げた。安定した構図が落ち着きをみせ，まわりを取り巻く
植物の緑の色も本体を殺さないように明度を考えて描いた。

Construction of Yata Hall for handicapped people
(Sanken Co., Ltd.)

A birds-eye view was used so that the entire structure
of the hall and its environment could be included in the
perspective. A stable composition was chosen to
calmly express the subject. To avoid spoiling the
sketch, deep consideration was given to the colors
used for the surrounding trees.

京都コンピューター学院正面ロビー
（株式会社銭高組大阪支社）

このスケッチは広告宣伝用にも使われるため，
若い学生風の人物を多数描いて，動的な要素を表してみた。

Main lobby of the Kyoto Computer School
(Osaka Branch of Zenitaka-gumi Co., Ltd.)

Since this sketch was intended for publicity, many
students were drawn in to express an element of
dynamic movement in the sketch.

第 5 章 ｜ 住 宅

Chapter 5｜Residential houses

休暇住宅村
海の休暇住宅分譲計画
Resort residence village
Parceling-out plan of seaside resort residences

表現チェックポイント

太陽と緑に恵まれた環境をアピールするためのプレゼンテーションパースなので，正確さより雰囲気優先の仕上げとなる。一区画当たりの贅沢な広さや，植栽の多い様子を明るいタッチで表現するように努めた。

設計コンセプトポイント

依頼人には一番ゆとりのあるところをスケッチすることを提案して，商業広告に使用するための絵をA，B，Cの3光景画に分けて作画することになった。この場合，住宅そのものは各人自由選択されるものなので，夢をもたせる個性あふれるシンプルで感性あるデザインを心がけた。

Check point for mode of expression

This is a presentation perspective of an environment blessed with sunlight and greenery, so the emphasis is placed on the creation of the atmosphere rather than on the realism of the scene. Efforts were made to convey the luxury and spaciousness of the residence lot and surrounding greenery with a bright, cheerful touch.

Main point of design concept

It was proposed to the client to incorporate the most luxurious portions of the residence lot into the perspective, so paintings of three scenes, A, B and C, were chosen for the commercial advertising. Since the residences were to be purchased at the free option of the buyer, it was necessary to attract such buyers by presenting a perspective depicting simple and unique designs that arouse and elaborate the dreams that they hope to realize.

サイズ:360mm×615mm
Size:360mm×615mm

❶構図を決めて本清書のペン線描画として完成させる。この段階で植栽の
プロポーションを整えてしまう。
❶ Decide the composition and finish the pen line drawing.
Decide the proportions of the plants in the drawing at this stage.

❷人物や車などマスキング液でふせる。
❷ Mask the people and cars using the masking liquid.

❸空と道路の着色をする。空には雲を浮かべ，同時に遠近感も考えて着
彩表現を終える。これは純粋絵画の世界と多少違った進め方になる。
❸ Color the sky and road. Draw clouds in the sky and color
them to express their depth and distance. Coloring clouds in
perspectives differs slightly from coloring clouds in non-com-
mercial, pure art painting.

❹道路の着彩表現を進める。木陰など描き終えたら，中央の人物をふせているマスキング液をラバーゴムでこすり取ってもよい。
❹ Color the road. After painting the shade of the trees, scrub off the masking liquid used to mask the people in the center of the painting with a rubber eraser.

❺次に住宅の描写にかかる。
❺ Next, draw the residence.

❻低木，遠景の樹林の表現も完成させる。
❻ Draw the bushes and trees in the far distance.

住宅マンション

山間部にある自然林に囲まれた閑静なメゾネット

Condominium

Maisonette-type condominium surrounded by a quiet forest

表現チェックポイント

構図は，右に傾斜した南面からの日差しやマイカーの出入口のある通路に重点をおいて描くことにした。この作品は短時間仕上げのスピードスケッチである。イメージ画は，いつも高級なキャンソンボードのみに描くものではなく，トレーシングペーパーに鉛筆による描写も多いが，イラストボード紙などのほうが作業能率がよい。着色する段になれば，なおさらである。

設計コンセプトポイント

イメージ段階での計画打診用スケッチなので，色調も単調な色に統一して着彩した。植物の葉の色も実際のグリーンをさけ，茶色でまとめてある。もちろん，依頼者とよく相談してのことである。

サイズ:352mm×680mm
Size:352mm×680mm

Check point for mode of expression

When deciding on the composition, the points chosen for highlighting were the south side of the condominium, which is inclined on the RH side under the sunlight, and the passage to the entrance to the parking lot. This perspective has a definite "sketchy" feeling, and was finished within a short period. Image paintings are not always drawn on deluxe Canson board; they are often drawn on tracing paper with a pencil. For the best efficiency in the preparation of such paintings, illustration boards are recommended. If the perspective is to be colored, illustration boards are more convenient.

Main point of design concept

Since the perspective was requested to study the project during the image creation stage, it was prepared with simple coloring and tones. Brown was used for the expression of the tree leaves, not green. This decision was of course made after careful discussion with the client.

❶住宅が落ち着いてみえるように，安定した構図をキャンソンボード（白）にペン線描画で仕上げる。

❶ To give the condominium a calm appearance, choose a stable composition drawn on a Canson board (white) for the line drawing.

❷淡彩塗りなので，マスキングなしで一般のスケッチ同様に，どんどん塗りこんでいく。塗りの順序は，特にない。

❷ Since it is to be finished in a light tone, continue coloring without the use of masking film as if you were making a normal sketch. No special order is required for applying the color.

❸一気に描き上げるためには，絵具を十分，手元に準備して作業すること。

❸ Prepare enough of the paint and colors before you begin painting so that you will be able to finish the perspective in one stretch.

❹一番濃い色は建物の影や植物の葉の色になるのだが，濃く塗り込みすぎないようにあっさり筆をおくこと。

❹ Though the darkest coloring portions in the perspective are the shade of the building and the leaves of the trees, take extra care not to make these portions too dark.

リゾート地のセカンドハウス

海抜25mの岸上の景勝地に建つ休暇住宅

Villa residence in a resort area

**Resort house constructed on the top of a seaside hill
25 meters above the sea level.**

クライアント:龍明デザイン事務所
サイズ:390mm×660mm
Client:Ryu Akira Design Office
Size:390mm×660mm

現場環境を含めて，計画案のおさまりを検討するため周辺環境をしっかり描き，建物のバランス，調子を構図の中におさめていく。ペン線描画で仕上げていくので，そのままでも十分なスケッチである。彩色，着色テクニックとして，ガラス面などはエアブラシで，その後手塗りによるグラデーション手法を駆使しながら，濃度の濃い段階まで塗り込んでいく。

設計コンセプトポイント

色彩コントロールの必要性がある作品。周辺の景色が強くなりすぎて，建物本体の調子が負けないように注意する。植物は緑と思い込まず，近景，中景，遠景の三拍子を忘れないように。遠景になれば，空色の層を通してその物体は青味を帯びてくる。目的は，楽しい休暇住宅の完成を予想するスケッチであること。

Check point for mode of expression

The environment adjacent to the construction site was included in the perspective so that the perspective could be utilized in the study for finalization of the construction plan. When arranging the composition of the perspective, consideration was given to the balance of the building and the tone. Since the perspective was prepared as a pen line drawing, it can be utilized as a sketch as it is. A gradation method of airbrushing and subsequent manual coloring was used to color and fix the colors of the glass surface, and the darker colors were applied to a degree almost equivalent to the finished level.

Main point of design concept

This is a work which requires control of color. Extra care should be exercised not to stress the adjacent landscape, thus spoiling the building, which is the main theme of the perspective. Don't take it for granted that the plants are green. There are slight changes in the tones of the trees in the near, middle and far distance. The objects in the far distance have more of a bluish color due to the reflection of the blue sky. Keep in mind that the purpose of the perspective is to present the predicted as-built appearance of the comfortable and pleasant-looking resort house.

❶キャンソンボード（白）の上に設計案を定着させ，鉛筆で割りつけをする。

❶ Transcribe the design idea onto a Canson Board (white) and allocate the objects in the composition using a pencil.

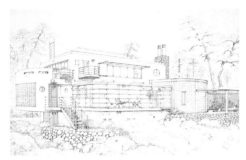

❷まず，ペン線描画として完成させてしまう。このままでも絵として完成しているところまで描く。

❷ First of all, finish the perspective as a pen line drawing. Proceed until the drawing of the perspective is almost finished.

❸薄い色で仕上げる場合，マスキングなしで空などをエアブラシで描いてもかまわない。岩場も土台の石積みもフリーに吹きつける。

❸ When finishing the perspective in lighter colors, you can finish the sky and other portions with an airbrush without using a masking film. Spray the colors freely over the rocks and masonry of the building foundation.

❹ただし，ガラス張り部分と窓部分は，画用紙全面をマスキングフイルムで
カバーし，カットして部分をはがし，エアブラシで吹きつけて着彩。奥行き
感もエアブラシと手塗りで表現する。ガラスブロックも，エアブラシのほうが
絵具のぼかしの美しいタッチが生きてくる。
❹ However, you must cover the drawing paper with the masking
film when you are finishing the glazed windows. After finishing
the windows, cut away the masking to prepare for subsequent
airbrush color spraying. The depth of the perspective can be
expressed by the airbrush and manual painting. Even when
finishing the glass block, color can be more effectively applied
with the airbrush to add a beautiful touch to the perspective.

❺絵全体の調子をつかむように，周囲の松や雑木林と低木を塗り込む。
❺ Finish coloring of the adjacent pine trees and the thicket of
assorted trees in consideration of the total color tone and
balance of the picture.

❻最後に，建物の付帯設備であるステップや煙突などの細かい部分の着
彩をすませる。
❻ Finally, place colors over the detailed portions of the picture
such as the stairs, chimney, and other accessories of the building.

セカンドハウス室内

温暖地に建つリゾートハウスのインテリア

Resort house

Interior of a resort house built in an area with a mild climate

表現チェックポイント

この構図は，ワンルームシステムを右（南面）に海をのぞめる一景として描くことが，ベストの表現だと決めた。この作品はていねいに表現したいため，エアブラシを多用して仕上げた。床木材フローリングの感じを出すにも，エアブラシ吹きつけと溝尺描写などを組み合わせて描いていく。また，家具，椅子テーブルは，提示された内容や姿をよくつかんで描写すること。調度品，ソファー，テーブルのバランスと表現が悪いと，室内全体の調子を悪くしてしまう。絵全体の明るさには，特に気を配った。

設計コンセプトポイント

依頼者から，図面上での説明と内装仕上げ材の質感や色調，家具類調度品のデザインを十分に伝達・説明してもらうことが必要である。なぜならば，表現の最終仕上げの調子とセンスは描き手（レンダラー）側の責任になるからである。この作品では人物描写をやめて静粛な落ち着きを出してみた。

Check point for mode of expression

This composition was considered to be the best to render the interior of one of the rooms in the resort house with a view of the sea on the right-hand side. An airbrush was frequently utilized in this perspective to carefully express the details of the interior. The combined application of the airbrushing and groove scale help to properly express the properties of the wooden flooring. Prior to drawing interior elements such as furniture, chairs and tables, you must have a clear understanding of their texture and forms, and of the requests that have been made by the client. Poor balance and poor expression of the furnishings, sofa and tables will spoil the total mood of the room. Extra care was exercised in drawing so that the picture became cheerful and bright.

Main point of design concept

Before starting the work, it is necessary for you to hear or get detailed instructions and description of the finish, texture, color tone and design of the furnishings, furniture and interiors to be installed. This is necessary because the renderer should take responsibility for the finish, tone and the sense of the perspective that he draws. No people were included in this perspective to create a mood of calm and repose.

クライアント:龍明デザイン事務所
サイズ:325mm×660mm
Client:Ryu Akira Design Office
Size:325mm×660mm

❶十分に構図バランスを検討して，鉛筆で本番描写にはいる。

❶ After allowing sufficient time to work out the composition and balance of the perspective, start the drawing with a pencil.

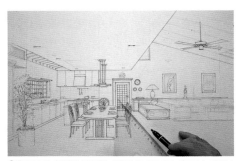

❷薄手の三角定規を片手で持ち，画面上にベタにおかずにスピードを出すためペンをそわせてラインを引く。

❷ Hold a thin triangle scale by one hand. Instead of placing the triangle scale entirely on the paper, lift one corner of the scale from the paper so that the pen line drawing can be made quickly.

❸床をきれいに着色するために，ダイニングテーブル，イスの脚などの色をつけたくないところにマスキング液を塗りふせる。面積の広い場合は，マスキングフイルムを使用すればよい。

❸ Use masking liquid to mask the portions of the perspective such as dining table and chairs which should not be colored at the initial stage. When the area to be masked is large, the use of masking film is recommendable.

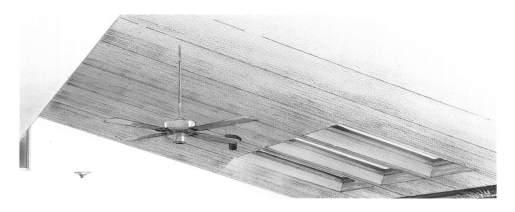

❹天井と床だけを着色する。1回目の色だけエアブラシで，あとはフリーハンドの溝さし定規とガラス棒，それに面相筆の大でコントラストをつける。

❹ color only the ceiling and the floor. Use an airbrush only when the initial coloring is made. The subsequent color contrast should be processed by a free hand using a groove scale, glass rod and a large line brush.

❺最後に，家具類の着色。ペンライト，天井扇風機，植木の順で進める。明るく快活な色調を出すことに専念する。

❺ Finally, color the furniture, pen lights, ceiling fan and plants in that order. Try to draw the perspective so that it can be finished in a bright and cheerful color tone.

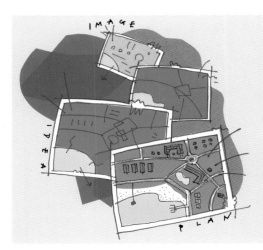

プレゼンテーションスケッチの役目

都市建設計画，市街地再開発計画などのすべての建築を考えるとき，作り手である建築家，計画グループと受け手である市民との間には，都市空間やその街並みの景観に対するイメージの共有がなければならない。

受け手である一般市民が一番知りたいのは，難解な建築の理論や主義ではなく，建築家や計画グループの内に広がるイメージの世界なのである。

Purpose of presentation sketches

When considering the many types of architecture employed in city planning, urban redevelopment projects, etc., it becomes clear that the architects and developers who develop the projects and the general citizens who are going to enjoy the final outcome of the projects should all share a common image of the city construction space and the landscaping incorporated in that city planning.

The general citizens who are going to use the proposed architectural space do not want to know about the difficult architectural theory or principles applied in the design process; they want a concrete image of what the architects and project planners are trying to build.

分譲マンション

ペン線描画で仕上げたのちに，彩色仕上げ。
生活感を出すために周囲に人物や車を配置した。

Condominium for sale

Colored in after a pen line drawing was completed. To
express the living atmosphere, the incidental people
and cars were arranged in the vicinity of the
condominium.

奈良県吉野町営住宅団地計画
（株式会社上田篤都市建築研究所）

山麓に位置する町営住宅計画。環境の良さも表現の
重要なポイントをしめた。

Local government-run housing complex plan in Yoshino Nara
（Ueda Atsushi Urban Design and Research Institute）

City-run housing complex which will be located at the
foot of a mountain. Expression of the environment was
one of the important objectives in the sketch.

高級分譲マンション

周辺の静寂な環境をPRしたい高級分譲マンション。
建物，手前の林ともペン画タッチで仕上げた。
描写の時間にゆとりがあった作品。

Deluxe condominium for sale

Since it was to be used for publicity, it was hoped that
the perspective would express the quiet surroundings
of the deluxe condominium. Both the building and the
forest in the foreground were finished by pen line
drawing. An ample time was allowed for the
preparation of this perspective.

マンションのリビングルーム
（株式会社AAA総合設計）

リビングルームとダイニングルームをのぞんだ構図。
木材のかもしだす暖かさと欧州的なムードを印象づけた。

Living room of a condominium
（AAA Sogo Design Co., Ltd.）

Composition featuring a living room and dining room.
Emphasis was placed on expressing the warm
atmosphere of the wooden furniture and objects to
create a European mood.

バー・ラウンジ

このようなスケッチは，人物を配置すると幼稚にみえてしまうことも
ある。この場合も人物がいないほうが風格を感じる。

Lounge in a bar

This type of perspective often looks amateur if people
are drawn in. This perspective presents the distinctive
mood of the bar without incidental people.

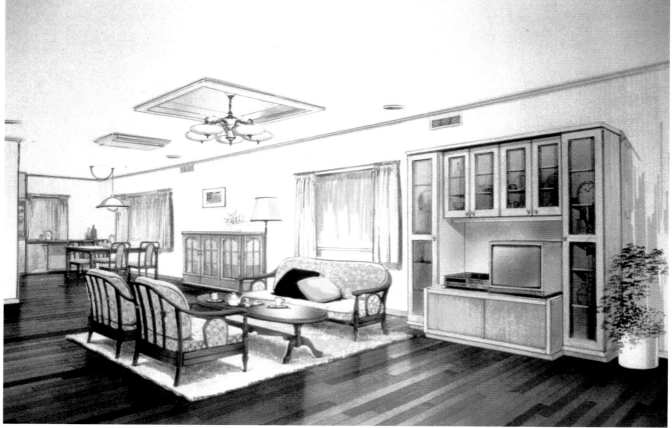

リビングルーム

木目のフローリングが特徴の贅沢なリビングルームなので，
調度品も木製品を配して描いた。木目のかもしだす暖かさを
表現するよう心がけた。

Living room

Since the living room featured luxurious wooden
flooring, wooden furniture was incorporated to enhance
the warm atmosphere of the wood grains.

第6章｜環境パースの主役達

人物／植物

Chapter 6｜Star players in the world of landscape perspectives

Human figures／Plants

人物のいろいろ

施設や環境スケッチのなかで，特に重要な役目を果たすのが人物である。さらに，人数，動き，そして配置しだいで雰囲気が大きく変わるので注意して，描きたいものである。それには，写生，デッサンを繰り返し演習して，自分なりのしっかりした人物の姿を描けるようにしておくことが大切である。

Draw various types of human subjects

Human subjects play the most important role in perspective sketches that present facilities and their environments. Since the atmosphere of a perspective can vary greatly with the number, movement and arrangement of the people included, you have to take extra care in rendering perspectives that involve people. To successfully do this, it is important to make numerous preliminary sketches and drawings of human subjects. You should establish your own way of expressing the humans included in your perspectives. You can draw any kind of pose or movement of your human subjects whenever you want.

❶歩行中の若い女性たち
専門店街などの通路，百貨店正面入口，エスカレータ前などでみられる近景として描くとき。
❶Young females walking
These young females are often drawn as incidental humans in the foreground of perspectives that present rows of specialty shops, main entrances of department stores, escalators, etc.

❷歩行中のビジネスマン
こちらにやって来る人物を「歩行中の若い女性たち」と同様に描き入れることで，より画面のアクション性が活気を出す。
❷Businessmen walking
Draw businessman who are coming in this direction in the same way as you drew the young females walking. This will add a vivid atmosphere to the drawing.

❸横に歩く人々
画面の単調さをさけるため描き入れたい。
❸People crossing in front of the illustrator
Put these people in the perspective to prevent the picture from becoming monotonous.

❹遠くへ行く人
遠ざかっていく人々の姿も，必ず描きたいもの。
❹People walking away from the illustrator
It is also advisable to sometimes include people walking away from you in your perspectives.

❺ちょっと先のほうでの立話中の人々
静止して会話中の人々も必ず入れる。雰囲気が作れる。
❺People chattering in the middle distance
Never fail to include people having enjoyable chats in the middle distance of your perspectives. These subjects will add to the atmosphere of the pictures.

スケッチ画の構図のバランスを，これら❶〜❺で示した基本的姿を描くことで，どっしりした安定感のあるパーススケッチとしてのインパクトをそなえることができる。

By drawing these fundamental human subjects described in steps ❶ through ❺ above, you can add balance to the compositions of your sketches and you can give your perspectives an impact with an imposing and well-balanced finish.

❻人待ち親子姿／親子連れ
横断歩道やスーパー入口付近
❻Parent and child/parties of parents and children
In pedestrian crossings or near supermarket entrances

❼広場，公園などで憩う家族連れ／戯れ遊ぶ子供たち，公園や空き地など
公共設備などの計画案のなかで，スケッチ描写の景観の中央に大きく表現しなければならないときが必ずある。よく学習しておくこと。
❼Families relaxing in plazas, parks and other places; children playing in parks or open spaces.
Since it is often necessary to draw these human subjects in the foreground of perspectives presenting public facilities, you should make a habit of frequently sketching them.

❻

❼

❽ウインドーディスプレーマネキン

静止しているが個性のある表情をしている。ウインドーが目の前に表現されるとき、ウインドー内のマネキンを下手に描いてしまうと、スケッチ全体に表現した他の設計コンセプト全体が幼稚にみえてしまう。重要なポイントとなるので人物も同様、日頃の学習演習が大切である。

❽ Mannequin displays in windows

They are perfectly motionless, but they have their own marked personalities to be expressed. If the mannequins in windows in the foreground are drawn inadequately, then the overall quality of the sketch, including the other design concepts that have been incorporated within it, is damaged; the end result looks amateur.

❾ホテルフロント／ホテルロビー／空港ロビー
❾ Hotel reception room/Hotel lobby/Airport lobby

❿会話中の人々（パーティなど）
❿ People chattering (at parties, etc.)

⓫オフィスレディ
⓫ Female office workers

⓬散策中の若い人々・公園プロムナード
⓬ Young people strolling along park promenades, etc.

⓭リゾート地など
⓭ Resort area

⓮ジョギング中の人々
⓮ People jogging

⓯ショッピングセンター／スーパーストアなど
生活感のある人々の動き
⓯ Shopping mall/Supermarket, etc.
The energetic movement of people in their daily lives

⓰見物中の親子
⓰ Parent and child spectators

⓱スポーツ，ゴルフをする人々
⓱ People playing golf

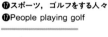

最も多く出てくる植樹, 街路樹, 公園樹のいろいろ

植物描写の演習練習は, 当然, 描く練習も必要になるが, その対象となる木々の
種類や特色を把握しておくことが求められる。そのためには, 日頃から, 公園などに
ある実物の木を観察し植物に親しむことが大切。

そのうえ, 木についている名札をみて名称を覚えることも忘れてはならない。また,
描くときに, 細部については専門の植物図鑑を必ず参考にすること。

Various types of plants, roadside trees and trees in parks which are often drawn in the sketches

When practicing your rendering of plants, it is natural that you should draw a variety of different types of plants and trees. It is also necessary for you to obtain sufficient knowledge about the parts and characteristics of the trees and plants you are going to draw. To do so, you should familiarize yourself with actual trees by always remembering to observe them whenever you get a chance to take a walk in a park or other such areas.

Moreover, it is also important for you to try to memorize the names of the trees described on the tags hung from the trees in the park. When you need to draw them, you should look them up in the existing reference literature. A good example of this type of reference material would be the "Book of Japanese Trees and Plants."

❶

❷メタセコイヤ／針葉樹（落葉）
公園樹・街路樹
❶Metasequoia Glyptostroboides Hu et Cheng (botanical name)／A needle-leaf tree (deciduous)
Park tree, Roadside tree

❷ケヤキ／広葉樹（落葉）
街路樹・公園樹・公共広場の緑陰樹・庭園樹・緑化樹
❷Zelkowa serrata Makino (botanical name)／A broadleaf tree (deciduous)
Roadside tree, Park tree, Tree for shade tree in public spaces, Garden tree, Greenery

❸アラカシ／広葉樹（常緑）
公園樹・庭園樹・街路樹・生垣用
❸Quercus glauca Thunb. (botanical name)／A broadleaf tree (evergreen)
Park tree, Garden tree, Roadside tree, Live fence tree

❹カツラ／広葉樹（落葉）
添景・街路樹・緑陰・景観樹・公園樹・庭園樹
❹Cercidiphyllum japonicum Sieb. et Zucc. (botanical name)／A broadleaf tree (deciduous)
Incidental items in painting, Roadside tree, Shade tree, Landscape tree, Park tree, Garden tree

❺イチョウ／針葉樹（落葉）
街路樹・公園樹
15～30mにもなる街路樹の王者。
❺Ginkgo biloba L. (botanical name)／A needle-leaf tree (deciduous)
Roadside tree, Park tree
The most popular roadside tree, sometimes growing as high as 15-30 meters

❻ラクウショウ／針葉樹（落葉）
公園樹・街路樹・庭園樹
特に洋風庭園に用いられる。
❻Taxodium distichum Rich. (botanical name)／A needle-leaf tree (deciduous)
Park tree, Roadside tree, Garden tree
Especially common in western-style gardens

❼トウカエデ／広葉樹（落葉）
公園樹・街路樹・庭園樹
❼Acer trifidum Hook. et Arn. (botanical name)／A broadleaf tree (evergreen)
Park tree, Roadside tree, Garden tree

❽クロガネモチ／広葉樹（常緑）
公園樹・庭園樹・街路樹
❽Ilex rotunda Thunb. (botanical name)／A broadleaf tree (evergreen)
Park tree, Garden tree, Roadside tree

❾クスノキ／広葉樹（常緑）
公園樹・街路樹
20～40m。日本産常緑樹で最も大きく。街路, 公園, 神社境内に必ずあり, 公共広場で親しまれる。
❾Cinnamomum Camphora Sieb. (botanical name)／A broadleaf tree (evergreen)
Park tree, Roadside tree
The tallest evergreen tree in Japan, growing from 20- 40 meters high. Often planted in public areas, on the roadside, and in parks, shrines, and temples.

❿クスノキ
5～6年の姿。
❿Cinnamomum Camphora Sieb. (botanical name)
A tree of five or six years old.

⓫アキニレ／広葉樹（落葉）
公園樹・庭園樹・街路樹
10～20mに成長する。
⓫Ulmus parvifolia Jacq. (botanical name)／A broadleaf tree (deciduous)
Park tree, Garden tree, Roadside tree. These trees usually grow from 10-20 meters high.

⓬マテバシイ／広葉樹（常緑）
公園樹・庭園樹・街路樹・生垣用
⓬Lithocarpus edulis Nakai (botanical name)／A broadleaf tree (evergreen)
Park tree, Garden tree, Roadside tree, Live fence tree

⓭ネズミモチ／広葉樹（常緑）
公園樹・生垣用
工場緑化などに用いられる。
⓭Ligustrum japonicum Thunb. (botanical name)／A broadleaf tree (evergreen)
Park tree, Live fence tree
Usually planted for greenery around plants and factories.

⓮シラカシ／広葉樹（常緑）
公園樹・街路樹・庭園用・生垣用
⓮Quercus myrsinaefolia Blume (botanical name)／A broadleaf tree (evergreen)
Park tree, Roadside tree, Garden tree, Live fence tree

⓯シイノキ／広葉樹（常緑）
生垣用・街路樹
⓯Castanopsis Spach. (botanical name)／A broadleaf tree (evergreen)
Live fence tree, Roadside tree

⓰キンモクセイ／広葉樹（常緑）
公園樹・庭園樹・生垣用
⓰Osmanthus fragrans Lour. var. aurantiacus Makino (botanical name)／A broadleaf tree (evergreen)

❷

❸

Park tree, Garden tree, Live fence tree

⓱カナメモチ／広葉樹（常緑）
公園樹・庭園樹・生垣用
⓱Photinia glabra Max. (botanical name)／A broadleaf tree (evergreen)
Park tree, Garden tree, Live fence tree

⑱コブシ／広葉樹（落葉）

庭園樹・公園樹・街路樹
公共広場の緑陰用。

⑱Magnolia kobus DC. (botanical name)/A broadleaf tree (deciduous)

Garden tree, Park tree, Roadside tree
A shade tree for public plazas.

---

⑲イヌツゲ／広葉樹（常緑）

公園樹・庭園樹
特に刈り込みの根締め用。

⑲Ilex crenata Thunb. (botanical name)/A broadleaf tree (evergreen)

Park tree, Garden tree
For planting in empty areas around the roots of trimmed trees.

---

⑳ホルトノキ／広葉樹（常緑）

公園樹・街路樹・庭園樹

⑳Elaeocarpus sylvestris Poir. var. ellipticus Hara (botanical name)/A broadleaf tree (evergreen)

Park tree, Roadside tree, Garden tree

㉑アオギリ／広葉樹（落葉）

公園樹・庭園樹・街路樹

㉑Firmiana platanifolia Schott et Endl. (botanical name)/A broadleaf tree (deciduous)

Park tree, Garden tree, Roadside tree

㉒フサアカシア／広葉樹（常緑）

街路樹・公園樹・庭園
特に洋風庭園に利用される。

㉒Acacia decurrens Willd. var. dealbata F. V. Muell. (botanical name)/A broadleaf tree (evergreen)

Roadside tree, Park tree, Garden tree
Most commonly planted in western-style gardens in Japan.

㉓イロハモミジ／広葉樹（落葉）

庭園樹・公園樹
和風庭園のポイントとして使われることが多い。

㉓Acer palmatum Thunb. (botanical name)/A broadleaf tree (deciduous)

Garden tree, Park tree
Often planted as a centerpiece tree in Japanese-style gardens.

㉔アメリカフウ／広葉樹（落葉）

街路樹・公園樹・庭園樹

㉔Liquidambar styraciflua L. (botanical name)/A broadleaf tree (deciduous)

Roadside tree, Park tree, Garden tree

㉕ヤブツバキ／広葉樹（常緑）

庭園樹・公園樹・生垣用

㉕Camellia japonica L. (botanical name)/A broadleaf tree (evergreen)

Garden tree, Park tree, Live fence tree

㉖サザンカ／広葉樹（常緑）

庭園樹・公園樹・生垣用

㉖Camellia Sasanqua Thunb. (botanical name)/A broadleaf tree (evergreen)

Garden tree, Park tree, Live fence tree

㉗オオシマザクラ／広葉樹（落葉）

公園樹・街路樹・庭園樹
公共広場の緑陰樹。

㉗Prunus speciosa Nakai. (botanical name)/A broadleaf tree (deciduous)

Park tree, Roadside tree, Garden tree
Usually planted as a shade tree in public areas.

㉘クヌギ／広葉樹（落葉）

公園樹・庭園樹・街路樹

㉘Quercus acutissima Carruth. (botanical name)/A broadleaf tree (deciduous)

Park tree, Garden tree, Roadside tree

㉙キリシマツツジ／広葉樹（常緑）

公園樹・庭園樹
オフィスビルの正面植え込みなどに用いる。別名クルメツツジ。

㉙Rhododendron obtusum Planch (botanical name)/A broadleaf tree (evergreen)

Park tree, Garden tree
Often planted as plantation in front of office buildings. Another name: Azalea Kurume.

㉚クルメツツジ／広葉樹（常緑）

公園樹・庭園樹
キリシマツツジの別名。オフィスビル玄関に用いる。

㉚Azalea Kurume (botanical name)/A broadleaf tree (evergreen)

Park tree, Garden tree
Another name for Rhododendron obtusum Planch. Often planted in front of office buildings.

㉛ドウダンツツジ／広葉樹（落葉）

庭園樹・公園樹・生垣用

㉛Enkianthus perulatus C.K. Schneid. (botanical name)/A broadleaf tree (deciduous)

Garden tree, Park tree, Live fence tree

㉜フッキソウ／常緑性

平地面を覆うように植込みするのに用いる。

㉜Pachysandra terminalis Sieb. et Zucc. (botanical name)/An evergreen tree

Usually planted to cover flat ground.

㉝クサツゲ／広葉樹（常緑）

公園樹・庭園樹
半日陰にたえるカバー用。

㉝Buxus microphylla Sieb. et Zucc. var. microphylla (botanical name)/A broadleaf tree (evergreen)

Park tree, Garden tree
Usually planted for covering the ground. Can survive under semi-shade conditions.

㉞ヒイラギナンテン／広葉樹（常緑）

庭園樹・公園樹・低木強陰樹
マンション玄関などの日陰に多い。

㉞Mahonia japonica DC. (botanical name)/A broadleaf tree (evergreen)

Garden tree, Park tree, A shrub which can survive in complete shade
Often planted in the shade around main entrances to condominiums.

㉟カンツバキ／広葉樹（常緑）

庭園樹・公園樹
１～1.5mに成長する。都市環境にもたえる生命力の強い木。

㉟Camellia hiemalis Nakai (botanical name)/A broadleaf tree (evergreen)

Garden tree, Park tree
These trees usually grow from one to one and a half meters tall. Can survive when planted in industrial areas and under harsh conditions.

㊱アベリア／広葉樹（常緑）

公園樹・庭園樹・生垣用・道路
公共広場の緑化樹や散策遊歩道などに用いる。

㊱Abelia grandiflora Rehd. (botanical name)/A broadleaf tree (evergreen)

Park tree, Garden tree, Live fence tree, Roadside tree
Usually planted as greenery in public areas or along walking paths and roads.

㊲ライラック／広葉樹（落葉）

公園樹・庭園樹
花の咲く木としての利用。

㊲Syringa vulgaris Linn. (botanical name)/A broadleaf tree (deciduous)

Park tree, Garden tree
These trees bloom seasonally.

㊳タマリュウ／常緑性

平地面・傾斜面のカバー用
自動車道のグリーン地帯などに使用。

㊳Ophiopogon japonicus Ker-Grawler f. nanus Hort. (botanical name) evergreen

Usually planted to cover flat or sloped ground, or as greenery along roads for automobiles.

㊴ハナミズキ／広葉樹（落葉）

公園樹・街路樹・庭園樹
６～７mに成長する。アメリカの代表的な花木として有名。

㊴Cornus florida L. (botanical name)/A broadleaf tree (deciduous)

Park tree, Roadside tree, Garden tree
Usually grow 6-7 meters tall. Well known as a typical US flower-blooming tree.

㊵ボウガシ／広葉樹（常緑）

公園樹・街路樹
アラカシのこと。庭園用として使用するものをボウガシと呼び、直列植樹しやすいのが特徴。マンション敷地内などに多用される。

㊵Boh oak (Another name for Quercus glauca Thunb. (botanical name) A broadleaf tree (evergreen)

Park tree, Roadside tree
When these trees are planted as garden trees, they are usually called "Boh" oak. These trees are readily transplanted. Often planted near condominiums.

⑳ ㉑

㉒ ㉓

㉕

⑲

⑱

❹サルスベリ／広葉樹（落葉）

庭園樹・公園樹

❹Lagerstroemia indica L. (botanical name)/A broadleaf tree (a deciduous tree)

Garden tree, Park tree

❷プラタナス／広葉樹（落葉）

街路樹・公園樹

公共広場の緑化樹。都市や町並みに多くみられる。

❷Platanus occidentalis L. (botanical name)/A broadleaf tree (deciduous)

Roadside tree, Park tree
Often planted as greenery in public areas, and often seen in urban areas.

❸ユリノキ／広葉樹（落葉）

街路樹・公園樹・庭園樹

洋風では主要な樹種の1つ。高さ20〜30mにもなる。

❸Liriodendron Tulipifera L. (botanical name)/A broadleaf tree (deciduous)

Roadside tree, Park tree, Garden tree
One of the most popular trees in Europe and USA, usually growing from 20-30 meters tall.

❹カイズカイブキ／針葉樹（常緑）

公園樹・街路樹・庭園用・生垣用

学校正門や公園に最もポピュラーに使われている。

❹Juniperus chinensis L. var. Kaizuka Hort. (botanical name)/A needle-leaf tree (evergreen)

Park tree, Roadside tree, Garden tree, Live fence tree
Often planted in front of the main gates of schools or in parks.

❺ワシントンヤシ／特殊樹

街路樹・公園樹

洋風庭園に用いられる。最近、開放的な南の海辺を連想されるこの種が，ペンションやマリンレジャーなどのスケッチに多く用いられている。

❺ Washington filifera H. Wendl. (botanical name)/Special species

Roadsde tree, Park tree
Often planted in western-style gardens. Recently, these types of palm trees are frequently drawn in sketches of pensions or marine leisure facilities to remind us of the tropical seaside.

❻トウジュロ／特殊樹

庭園樹・公園樹

西日本に多い。南国風な姿が好まれる。潮風にも強い。

❻Trachycarpus wagnerianus Becc. (botanical name)/ Special species Garden tree, Park tree

Often seen in the western part of Japan. These trees have been popular for their tropical mood.
Can survive in areas prone to strong coastal winds.

❷

❸

❹

❹

❺

❻

植栽の描写実例

街路樹としてケヤキを描く，ふつう植樹後 7 〜 8 年先の姿で表現する。
Draw several "Keyaki"s (Botanical Name: Zelkowa serrata
Makino) as roadside trees seven or eight years after they have
been planted.

植樹後 7 〜 8 年。十分葉をつけたケヤキ。
Rows of seven- or eight-year-old "Keyaki"s with ample leaves

住宅街に植樹されたホルトノキ。
Elaecarpus sylvestris Pir. var. ellipticul Hara（botanical name）
planted in residential area

あ　と　が　き

エスキースから生まれてくる限りないアイデアやデザインソースを大切に頭の中にもストックし，いざ本番の机上であれこれ躊躇せず，線描開始時に添景配置のセンスある構図構成や着色の手順や調子が連鎖反応してくるように，常日頃から怠らずに練習することが一番大切です。

パースは写生画ではありません。まだ実在していない景観を想像しながら描くものなのです。ですからどのように描くかより，どのような見え方，おさまり方になるかを頭の中で繰り返して立体空間を描き，それらの建物や施設設備が実際に完成したときの周辺環境との調和を考えつつ，描き上げなくてはなりません。

透視図法はもちろんのこと，簡単な作画方法である一消点透視図法，二消点透視図法，三消点透視図法なども，常に駆使され活用されています。本書では，透視図法にはくわしく触れておりません。あくまで別途勉強として，おのおの努力してください。自分を取り巻く実在している街並みを被写体としてとらえ，見る角度，時間，光っているものやほかのものへの映り込みなどをよくスケッチブックに写し取り，訓練しておくことが，パーススケッチ作画のテクニックの上達の早道です。

建築本体の内部空間に展開されるショッピングセンターになると，とても複雑なもので，建築本体意匠や造作を描き込むだけではなく，その環境と臨場感までをも表現しなくてはなりません。流行のハイファッション，グレードの高い有名デザイナーの服飾品，ガラススクリーン内に見える煩雑なハンガーの陳列，そして動的に行きかう人物たち，中庭に見えるベンチ，植物，若者の群れ，大天井からトップライトの光が射し込んでいる営業中のムードまで描かないと，計画の最終受け手側であるクライアントを理解，感動させることはできません。

コンピュータグラフィックスが発達した今日でも，空気を通して見えるようなソフトな描写が表現できるフリーハンドスケッチの存在価値は，とても重宝なものです。

インテリアデザイン，ショップデザイン，百貨店内装飾，そして飲食レストランなどの計画プランのスケッチがつくられるとき，一般建築設計計画などとは違い，非常に短いサイクルで発想からデザイン決定，施工までと展開されていきますが，それを短期間に，しかもバラエティに富んだ要素が盛り込まれていなければなりません。最初は何種類かの構想をもってアプローチされ，最終的に一案に絞り込まれていくのですが，一つのスケッチを描くとき，私たちのデスク上には時間的猶予はなく，瞬間スピードが要求されます。一刻も速く計画意図を相手側に理解してもらいたい，その一心でスケッチ表現に全力を注ぐ切迫感がテクニックの上達の大きな要因ともいえるでしょう。

さらに，プレゼンテーションスケッチといっても，正確な構造表現，質感表現，そして絵画的に展開する空間の広がりなど，臨場感ある画風に仕上げていく心がまえを忘れてはいけません。

1994年10月吉日

龍　明

エスキーススケッチの繰り返しで
色々な空間がよく見えてくる

The repetition of esquisse sketches will bring a variety of spaces to view

It is important to keep accumulating the numerous ideas and design sources which are generated through the repeated drawing practices of esquisse sketches. In this way, ideas can emerge spontaneously when they are needed. The ideas reflected in the composition, the arrangement of incidental items and the coloring arrangement, can inspire the artist when beginning the line drawing.

A perspective is not a realistic painting of objects. It is an imaginary drawing of what does not actually exist. Therefore, it is not the matter of how and what to draw, but a matter of how to present three dimensional space (which has so far been only conceived) so that the viewers can grasp the image of what the building or facilities will be like when they are actually completed. And in drawing a perspective, it is also important to consider the balance between the theme of the structure and the environment in which the structure will be completed. In addition to basic perspective technique, one–point linear, two–point linear and three–point linear perspective methods have often been used. In this book, the perspective technique has not been explained in detail. I strongly hope that you will find an opportunity to study this as well. Try to draw any kind of object that can be regularly seen in daily life from various angles at different times of the day. Try to practice sketching shiny surfaces or the reflection of objects. This basic exercise is the fastest way to master perspective sketching technique.

The developed space within a shopping mall is extremely complicated, and in order to express it, it is necessary to draw not only the architectural characteristics of the shopping mall and the interior, but also the environment and the feeling of being present at the scene. In order to ensure that the client will understand, appreciate, and approve the perspective sketch, it is imperative to include such elements as the latest high fashion outfits designed by noted designers, rows of displays seen through the glass screen, the movement of people, benches in the patio, plants, groups of young people standing around, and the light from the skylight illuminating the shops and enhancing the mood and activity within them.

Even today, with the great progress of computer graphics, freehand sketches executed with a soft touch, the kind of touch that can actually be seen in real life, are still invaluable in the development process for a project.

When perspective sketches for interior designs, shop designs, department store interiors, restaurant construction plans, etc., are to be drawn, the entire process, from the creation of the initial idea to the more concrete decisions on the design and method of construction, is a process which must incorporate numerous factors, and which must be finished a short period. This process differs from that applied to general architectural design sketches, which of course allows a longer preparation period. The approach addressed in this book begins with the study of several ideas, and then gradually narrows them down into a more simple, unified idea. The time allowed for the illustrator to draw the sketch, however, is quite limited. To present the sketch to the client as quickly as possible to help the client understand the intention of the project, the illustrator must put forth his best effort. This effort will result in the improvement of his sketch drawing technique.

Always keep in mind that even when drawing a sketch for a presentation, the structure, the texture and the expansion of the aesthetic space of the objects should be precisely expressed so that the viewer a sense of being present in the scene.

Akira Ryu, October 1994

りゅう あきら
龍 明

1934年福岡県久留米市に生まれる。
県立明善高等学校を卒業後,
福岡市飲食産業企業企画宣伝部をへて,
商業建築設計事務所に従事。
1970年ファッション関係クライアンツを得て
龍 明デザイン事務所設立。
イメージパース, スケッチ表現の多い性質上
ついパース作画専門アトリエとなり現在に至る。

龍 明デザイン事務所
〒541 大阪府大阪市中央区北久宝寺町2-6-10
ニューライフ船場1502
電話:06-251-6023 FAX:06-251-6045

建築環境パース 実践技法
The Best Use of Landscape Items in Architectural Rendering

発行	**1994年11月25日　初版第1刷発行**
著者	**龍 明**（ⒸAkira Ryu）
装丁	**箕浦 卓**
本文デザイン	**箕浦 卓** 協力： 金久保文枝＋佐々木悦子
企画編集	**大田 悟**
翻訳	**株式会社バベル・インターナショナル**
コラム・イラスト	**火取ユーゴ**
校正	**アレフ**
発行者	**久世利郎**
発行所	**株式会社グラフィック社** 〒102 東京都千代田区九段北1-9-12 谷内ビル Tel.03-3263-4318 Fax.03-3263-5297 郵便振替・00130-6-114345
印刷・製本	**錦明印刷**株式会社
デザイン写植	**イノックス**

乱丁・落丁はお取り替え致します。
ISBN4-7661-0771-3 C3052